Life Was Like That Only

Prabeen Singh, who lives in Delhi, has had a varied career and many incarnations: a vocation in the women's movement, starting out as an activist in Saheli; as a development consultant, working with international agencies and later in the field of HIV/AIDS in North-East India; as a founder-member of the artisans' collective Dastkar; and as writer of a newspaper column on etiquette and food. Her current avatar is as a cook, teaching cooking classes in Delhi and conducting demonstrations/lectures for groups visiting India and seeking an insight into Indian food and culture. Well known for her personal style and hospitality, Prabeen Singh has written and lectured on aspects of Indian cuisine and appeared on India's top lifestyle channel NDTV Food. This is her first book.

Life Was Like That Only

PRABEEN SINGH

LIMITED
EDITIONS

First published in 2016
by
LIMITED EDITIONS
an imprint of

ACADEMIC FOUNDATION

Delhi Sales Office:
4772-73 / 23 Bharat Ram Road,
(23 Ansari Road), Darya Ganj,
New Delhi - 110 002 (India).
Phones : 23245001 / 02 / 03 / 04.
Fax : +91-11-23245005.

Corporate Office:
No. 35, Sector 7,
IMT Manesar,
Gurgaon - 122050.
Haryana (India).
Tel: +91-124-4215070 / 71.

E-mail : books@academicfoundation.com
www.academicfoundation.org

Disclaimer:
The findings/views/opinions expressed in this book are solely those of the author and do not necessarily reflect the views of the publisher.

Photographs appearing in the book have been duly credited to the source/copyright holder(s) wherever applicable.

Cataloging in Publication Data--DK
Courtesy: D.K. Agencies (P) Ltd. <docinfo@dkagencies.com>

Singh, Prabeen, author.
Life was like that only / Prabeen Singh.
pages cm

ISBN 9789332703827

1. Singh, Prabeen. 2. Life. I. Title.

BD431.S56 2016 DDC 113.8 23

Printed and bound by The Book Mint, New Delhi.
www.thebookmint.in

For

Nikhat and Pratap

Contents

Preface

"The moving finger writes: and having writ, moves on."
(Omar Khayyam, *The Rubaiyat*)

Life is movement. Nothing is static or absolute. We are in a state of constant flux, just as is the earth, the tides, light, the blood that courses through our bodies, colours, and so much else. Curiously, the only thing life guarantees is continuing evolution and, eventually, the 'white light'. So it is with memories.

I wrote this book to paint pictures of my life that I could glance through, just as one does with albums of photographs but through words rather than images. I wrote it for my family, now and in the future, my friends, and others who would recognise in my memories, some of their own, and observe some reflections of themselves. Photographs are revealing and bring to life memories but they cannot tell the underlying story, the context of events beyond our own, and how they impacted our own experiences.

Delhi
October 2016

Prabeen Singh

Acknowledgements

This book has been motivated, influenced, and shaped by many members of my family and friends, so I am immensely grateful to:

My literary 'enforcer,' Malvika Singh, who believed I could write, and when I didn't, persevered until I actually did.

My crazy, passionate, opinionated family, Baljeet Mehra, Ashwath and Malika Mehra, and Nancy Singh, who surrendered their version of the truth, occasionally bouncing off their memories against mine.

My elder brother and lifetime nemesis, Surinder Singh, very special thanks for joining me on this journey of 'mutual catharsis'.

My 'perennials', Pincha Singh, Farida Ali, Jyoti Moolgavkar, for sharing precious secrets and memories over a lifetime.

Ritu Menon, Roopa Mehta, Rachna Pasricha, and Neera Batra, my Vinay Marg cabal.

My friends, Suman and Manju Dubey, Malini Saran, Minty and Mintu Pande, Aruna Sultan, Mallika and M.J. Akbar, Yashodara Dalmia and Masseh Rehman, Alkha Dalmia, Sunil, Shalini, and Jivi Sethi, Michael Aram, Shashi Singh, Uzra Bilgrami, Simi and Sayed Zaidi, Brigitte Singh, Bharati Sharma, Christine, and Aman Rai, Salman and Kusum Haider, Shika Trivedi Singh, Tejbir Singh, Neelam Deo, Poonam Mutreja and A.K. Shiva Kumar, Pogey Menon, Madhu and Krishnan Jain, Madhu Khanna, Paula Manfredi, Syeda Imam, and Laila Tyabji, all of whom have inspired, guided, scolded, and protected me for over four decades.

Ajai and Shiromani Singh for taking me back to the days of the Janata Party and the Mandal agitation.

Razia Grover, for her encouragement, patience, comments, and valuable insights.

Nirad Grover for walking me through the Asian Games.

My godchildren: Karan Singh, Trishna Singh, Tahir Sultan, Zahed Sultan, Nadir Sultan, Girija Shivakumar,

Ishan Shivakumar, Shruti and Rahul Reddy. You are the bright lights.

Adil Tyabji, who helped to refine my book and exchanged his craft for homemade marzipan.

My spirit world: Ajeet Kaur, Rabindar Singh, Moni Singh, Uday Himmat Singh, S.P. Singh, Jyoti Baswan, Ghazi Sultan, Asha Dalmia, Ashok Batra, Ajit Saran, Gigi Noia, Asgari Imam, Zamir Ansari, Bunny Page, and John Andrew Wolohojian.

October 2016 Prabeen Singh
New Delhi

- 1 -

Jamshedpur

Jamshedpur, my beloved Tata Nagar — encountering these names unexpectedly in the newspaper or very rarely in an article makes me pause for that one precious moment when the innocence of my childhood races through the visual third eye — images making way for sounds, smells, and a profound yearning to return in time and once again become the 'Nini Baba' of my most beloved Sundari Amma, or ayah as she was generally referred to.

I was born in Jamshedpur, or Tata Nagar, as it was better known as the home to the Tata Iron & Steel Company. While not exactly a company town, the city benefited from the well-known social largesse of the Tata family. Hospitals, parks, social clubs, and the like all bore the name Tata this and Tata that. My father, Rabindar

Singh, newly returned from university in America, got his first job at the National Metallurgical Laboratory in Jamshedpur. His time in America is, in itself, an interesting sidelight. In any event, off he went on a US troopship from Calcutta with a shipload of American servicemen being repatriated at the end of the war at a time when the Atlantic was still swarming with German submarines. He left behind his extended family, his wife, and an eighteen day old son, Surinder my elder brother.

My father brought home a literal shipload of memories which became the stuff of his conversation throughout his life. Invariably happy memories barring the familial separation. I remember leafing through *Collier's* and the *Saturday Evening Post* magazines, to which he had subscribed before leaving America. These cultural introductions were augmented for our family by the importation of a flotilla of 'experts' from Pittsburgh to assist in the expansion of Tata's steel mills in Jamshedpur. It was indeed a 'Yankee' invasion. We lived in the Circuit House area, where most of the expatriates chose to live, and their children went to the local schools. Girls went to Sacred Heart Convent (all girls after third grade) and boys went to St Loyola's School. Johnny Stepanik was

My mother, Ajeet Kaur, and elder brother, Surinder Singh, Lahore, 1946.

My father, Rabinder Singh as a student in America.

a handsome kid, the proverbial blue eyes and blonde hair, and the absolute love of my life at the age of four. I sometimes wonder what became of my gladiator. We read American magazines and comic books, and listened to American music. Food was another revelation. Hot-dogs, hamburgers, macaroni all carried a certain gourmet aura and the reciprocal offering of samosas, pakoras, and kababs were not embraced with fervour by our newly-acquired friends. It was an almost magical time of life. Friendships and freedom flourished. After school, swimming lessons at the Beldih Club followed by free peanuts at 6 p.m. with a gaggle of kids hovering around anxiously for their share. Movies, usually in English, on weekends at the Golmuri Club, sitting on the carpeted lawn with ice cream dripping all over us. Running in and out of each others' homes accompanied by battleaxe ayahs, picnics with a cluster of families, dinner parties at home with parents all decked up while we watched the proceedings from the upstairs balcony, eyes wide open and mouths agape in wonderment.

I close my eyes and see myself with my two brothers, one four years older, the other younger by an equal number of years. The three of us would lie on our stomachs, chins propped up on palms, minutely observing my mother, Ajeet Kaur, readying herself for a dinner party. She would sit at her dressing table (the one with a three-way mirror) and slowly begin the ritual of 'putting together her public face', as she called it. All three of us understood that this was a very serious business, or, as she would say, 'Shringar Raas: my meditation'. No hurried gestures from her, and not a squeak from us. Even my hyper-kinetic younger brother Moni would remain transfixed and goggle-eyed. First she matched her glass bangles with her sari, curling her fist, gently pushing them towards her wrist, clinking their way to her arm. Each gesture so imbued with grace that my elder brother would describe it many years later 'as the flutter of a butterfly'. From removing the crimping clips in her hair to the final phase. Turning the mirror in all directions, she sprayed herself with her favourite perfume, while the three of us anticipated an approaching aromatic whiff. Then she pinned two fragile *motia* flowers hanging on a stem with just one leaf on the left side of her bun. She would then look at us with a wicked smile and proclaim: 'The war paint is on; go tell your father to stop sulking. I am only 18 minutes late.'

She would clickety-clack down the stairs, rolling out instructions to Amma to immediately put us to bed, little realizing that our very own 'party' awaited us, or at least for my elder brother and me. My younger brother usually fell asleep before the 'ritual' was over and had to be carried to bed.

My brother and I would sit on our favourite chairs in the veranda adjoining the garden, with our 'durbar' sitting cross-legged or on their haunches. A wonderful session of ghost stories would then ensue. The *mali* and the cook's helper, Jaggu, would compete for our attention: the gorier the story, the better. We travelled into dark rooms full of monsters, headless bleeding bodies, *churails* hanging from pipal trees, their feet *ulta*, waiting to lure unsuspecting men. Each storyteller swore on some imaginary aunt or a long dead relative (playing safe.) that they had actually witnessed all they narrated. Midway into our session, the cook, Shambu, would walk in with a helping of the dessert he had saved for just this occasion. We welcomed the treats but knew he would sternly order our *praja*, which included the chowkidar, to get back to work, even admonishing Amma for allowing us listen to such nonsense. It was all a question of balance of power: he allowed us our 15 minutes, served the treat, and then broke up the party.

We lived a life replete with routine: a timetable which dictated when we got up on schooldays, had our breakfast supervised by the cook and Amma, while our mother peacefully and leisurely sipped her tea in bed. Playtime, homework time, study time, and extra reading or hobby time. Then followed the magical 30 minutes before dinner when the five of us sat down and listened to wonderful music. None of us cared for the melancholy sounds of the *shehnai* or Chopin or ghazals, my mother's favourites, but perked up and danced to Mahalia Jackson, Billie Holliday, Duke Ellington ... I just loved listening to *Cherry Pink and Apple Blossom White*, and Eddie Calvert certainly had way of making a trumpet sound like a human being. Dinner, the family meal, was always at 6 p.m. in winter and 7 p.m. in summer. A lively discussion followed on that one special thing that had happened to each of us that day. As life was not always an adventure, we would invent incidents, each well aware that the other was 'make-believing'. In this we were wholeheartedly encouraged by our parents who believed that these were not to be considered 'white lies' but our creativity being given full rein. My father's stories were always rooted in the political news of the day and my mother would relate another nature story for us to digest and remember. Dinners were special because we received our parents' undivided attention, and that was sheer joy because they would often be going out later.

My surreptitious lunch dates every afternoon in Amma's room were equally special. The coarse red rice, soaked and fermented overnight, eaten with an onion, green chilli, and a few drops of mustard oil (*panto bhat*). This was usually accompanied by tiny deep-fried fish, a repast which, in my eyes, was far superior to anything at my mother's table. I silently heard the cook and Amma reminiscing about their families left behind in their Santhal villages, and about the school and college that were being built by the Tatas. They were convinced that none of the children who would be studying in that school could ever hope to become the big babu: '*Sab* assembly-line *banenge*'. The sentence sounded strange and musical to my ears and I used it to express just about anything that displeased me, much to my parents' amusement.

All three of us were aware of an uneasy air in the household which my brother called 'not quite routine'.

This was a phrase my younger brother and I were unable to fathom, although we all sensed my mother's deep undercurrent of distress and a very tightly controlled tension between my parents. Some nights we would awake to the sound of loud angry voices and harsh words being exchanged. The morning after, another 'sunny' day, but we lived with an uneasy sense of disquiet.

I will never forgot the day my father returned from office loaded with tins of Ovaltine, Kraft cheese, biscuits, chocolates, and a host of other goodies, loudly remarking: 'Revolution is round the corner; all edibles will be scarce.' He had blown up his entire pay packet stocking up on (mostly American) sweetmeats and savouries. My mother shouted, that these were so irrelevant at a time when we were living in a state of siege. How ironical and this for one who professed to be a diehard Communist. She was furious at what she called his hypocritical ways and his complete lack of any financial sense. 'If there was a revolution,' she loudly stated, 'the children should learn to be happy living the way eighty per cent of the children live in independent India. Deprived indeed.' In truth, that was exactly why my father himself expected a peasant revolt to erupt and be joined by factory workers' unions. We three children were left to salivate at the 'goodies' which were promptly returned to the store, but revolution became a much used word with my younger brother who showed early characteristics of an anarchist playing the angry peasant or a trade unionist. We acquired a whole new vocabulary, avidly imbibed by the elder brother from various Soviet magazines to which my father subscribed and then spewed out at us.

My parents' social calendar was always full as Tata Nagar had a large contingent of German and American expats. Many were consultants attached to Tata Steel, others assisted in building a state of art hospital largely funded by the Tatas. I recall an occasion when my elder brother silently sneaked into the kitchen and gobbled up all the six pomfrets intended to form the main course at my parents' dinner party. The cook hysterically showed my mother six very neat pomfret skeletons. This time my parents' sense of humour entirely deserted them.

Surinder and I had a special machaan: a wooden railing which was linked to the banister on the first floor providing us with a birds-eye view of the adults. My most cherished 'viewing' was the sight of the most beautiful woman in the world, my mother's friend. She wore a

The expats in a desi avatar, 1954.

backless blouse, a very flimsy saree, smoked, had dark red nail polish, and there were deep acne marks on her cheeks . . . I fervently prayed that I would one day look just like her. Notwithstanding acne marks, her glamour and elegance bewitched me. Among the guests would be a 'common law wife', my mother's closest friend, whom no one else invited. I had no idea what the term meant but like the acne-marked beauty with red nails, for me she spelt adventure.

Snakes were not uncommon sightings. We learnt how to distinguish between poisonous kraits and cobras, and garden- and rat-snakes. None of us, apart from the *mali* (who no one quite believed), had seen the king cobra and his mate. They apparently lived in a large mango tree, which also branched out into our neighbours' (Jesuit priests who taught my brothers) garden. We did however keep a safe distance from the danger area and harboured a genuine sense of collective fear. That was until one day when we heard a babel of loud voices in the garden and ran out to see what it was all about. A massive king cobra was sliding down the boundary wall and moving with great ferocity towards a squirrel transfixed by fear. My father ran for his .22 rifle only to be stopped short by my mother who asked him sternly what harm this beautiful creature had done to any of us. We needed to respect their territory and leave them alone. We all felt taller that day but I had snake nightmares for many months thereafter, and almost convinced my mother that I could actually see some. That continued until the day my aunt, with a doctoral thesis in clinical psychology, came to stay. She, in a truly Freudian manner, pronounced that snakes symbolized sexuality and I was unconsciously becoming aware of mine. At age 7. Needless to say, her prognosis did not sit well with my parents.

Further armchair analysis continued. That was especially true of the day she was awoken by a ruckus of excited young voices, and the desperate clucking of a hen. She rushed down to see that her niece and younger nephew were trying to decapitate a hen with a blunt knife (we had, as was common those days, our own poultry coop). I was holding on to her with a broad maniacal smile, or so she described the scene to my mother, and my brother, equally maniacal, was trying to behead the 'poor creature'. When asked why, we informed her that we wanted to see her run headless. Chickens have a great facility for running headless for a maximum of three minutes before their valiant hearts give way. My brothers and I would bet our week's pocket money on this ghoulish race. This memory of sibling bonding remains, perversely, one of my fondest. The cook would, early on Sunday morning (the only day on which, without persuasion, we got up at crack of dawn) select two free-range chickens from our small poultry shed. Amidst their loud clucking protest began the process of serving the 'bird' for our Sunday lunch. We would choose our own hens and bet on which would run faster and longer. I really do not recall ever betting on a horse and experiencing the same thrill when 'my side won'. My aunt was understandably horrified, more I think at my mother's (who had spent her childhood on a village farm) reaction that 'children will do such things'. From that day on she labelled us as a very dysfunctional family, and I honestly believe that to a degree she was correct.

I remember my father returning from America in the mid-1950s with two nylon sarees for my mother, who promptly rejected them as plastic and cheap. Word spread among her friends and beyond that she had sarees of the latest fabric: nylon. When I returned from a swim at the club I would see my mother entertaining strangers, friends, acquaintances. They would all be fingering the sarees in awe, overwhelmed with admiration that they did not need to be ironed. Never did I see my mother so defeated by social norms, obliged to entertain almost the entire population of women in Tata Nagar in extreme invasion of her privacy. We never again saw those sarees.

Another memory is of being crushed by the fury and physical violence of my elder brother, when he attempted to drag me back to our home from my best friend Farida's, who was also a neighbour. He kept screaming that in his history lesson that morning in his Jesuit school, St Loyola, the history teacher had told them that Muslims were our enemies and particularly the Mughal rulers: Aurangzeb had killed the Sikh guru Tegh Bahadur. The residual memory of a two-year old boy travelling on one of the last trains from Lahore to Delhi and witnessing the surrounding violence had raised its head. This became a recurring nightmare that would awaken him screaming: 'The Muslims are coming; they have torched the houses, we must run.' This would haunt him for many years. Hamida aunty and my mother returned from their coffee session to witness the ayahs shouting, the

The ghouls: with my younger brother Moni, Jamshedpur, 1955.

My aunt Dr Baljeet Mehra, many years later, in my flat in Vasant Vihar, New Delhi, 1982.

daughters crying, and my brother hysterical. From that day on my father began teaching my brother 'alternative' history, focusing on the rich diversity of our country where faiths, cultures, customs, and deities of all Indians must be respected and protected. It was a far cry from the factual textbook lessons being taught to the first generation of students in independent India in the so-called 'progressive' schools. I did not much understand it but vividly recall my mother recounting how ashamed and helpless she, along with my grandparents, felt, when the train carrying them to Amritsar was stopped by bloodthirsty Sikhs and Hindus. They entered the compartment with blood dripping from their swords searching for Muslims, and zeroed in on two young girls clinging to each other. Horrified by these monsters they pleaded, *'Khuda ki kasam hum Mussalman nahi hain'*. She said their screams reverberated forever in her ears, and enveloped her in a deep sense of shame.

I do not remember my parents ever being critical of Muslims or Islam, or grieving about the inanimate objects, land, or the homes they had left behind. Rather, they grieved the loss of many friends, a shared vocabulary, ambitions, loves, laughter, and tears. Their

best friends were our neighbours, Dr Syed Mehmood's daughter Hamida and her husband Syed Mohammed Naim, my Farida's parents. Dr Mehmood was a staunch Congress member and minister in the first cabinet. He and my grandfather had known each other well

My brother and I posing in Jamshedpur (behind that angelic smile he was plotting my downfall), 1951.

from the several National Congress sessions held in Lahore. We lived as an extended family, and in addition I insisted on learning the Koran from the *maulvi* when he came to instruct Farida. I was always intrigued by an oft-repeated question asked by aunty Hamida when they dined with us: '*jhatka ya halal?*' My mother would patiently remind them that 'we do not like the taste of *jhatka* mutton and our preference is always for *halal* meat.' Farida's explanation of the difference was vague and unsatisfactory. I did, however, overhear my Freudian aunt teasing my father about the two promises he had extracted from her before she went to London to work with Ms Anna Freud : 1. Never go to a pub, because young women from good families do not; 2. Do not think of marrying a Pakistani.

The year and date, 5 August 1956, stands out vividly in my memory. Back from school, I rushed into the family room anxiously inquiring whether Moni, my younger brother, was at home as he had got 'lost' the previous day (as the cook's nephew, who had been entrusted to 'walk' him in his stroller had lost his way home). There had in consequence been enormous hysteria, commotion, and mixed emotions, especially mine, as a part of me did wish him lost so that I could occupy centre stage. My question satisfactorily answered, I went to look for my mother, another daily routine, to find her removing all that was precious to us children from the family music room. I was assaulted by a flurry of spring-cleaning and was informed that my grandparents, Papaji and Bibiji, from Delhi were coming to stay with us for a month. The next week was spent on learning Punjabi etiquette. Every morning and evening the boys had to touch their feet and say 'Sat Sri Akal'. I, the daughter of the house, was not to ape my brothers and dive, but gracefully bow, I think she said at 30 degrees, and also say 'Sat Sri Akal'. Efforts to teach us Punjabi failed miserably, but we did learn the names of the 10 gurus and a 'shorthand' history of what it takes to be a Sikh. That left me a touch puzzled, as the nuns in my school had been teaching us how to be good Catholics and it all seemed the same. My elder brother was joyful because he, the cherished first-born, remembered his grandparents well from (as he loftily announced) United India days, whatever that meant. I had a vague memory of visiting them in Delhi as a two-year old, but my younger brother had no idea who Bibiji and Papaji were.

My grandfather, Principal Niranjan Singh.

A family portrait with my grandmother, Basant Kaur, Jamshedpur, 1953.

My father's bar was locked for 30 days and our weekend shikar trips to forests around Dimla Nala or Hazaribagh stopped. My mother's coffee parties and other activities were curtailed. However, every evening we had a stream of visitors. First just the Sikhs and Punjabis, then others who came to 'pay their respects' to my grandfather, Principal Sahib, and eager to touch his feet. It left my younger brother and me bemused to discover that virtually everyone in Tata Nagar was a relative, believing as we did that only the family could lay claim to feet touching. Ceaseless cups of tea, *nimbu-pan*i, pakoras, cakes, and sandwiches were whisked past our 'grabby' hands for these strangers. Partition, Lahore, Forman Christian College, Kinnaird, Sikh National College, Rawalpindi, Karachi, Gandhi, Nehru, Sardar Patel, Mountbatten, Baldev Singh, Syed Mehmood, Maulana Azad, Jinnah, Master Tara Singh, Dr Radhakrishnan, Kamaghata Maru, the Ghaddar Party, Subash Chandra Bose ... The names rolled on and sounded to my ears like different notes of a song wrapped in nostalgia, pride, pain, a deep sense of loss, new beginnings.

When I inquired from my mother why Papaji was

called Principal Sahib, I learnt that he had given up being a professor of chemistry at Forman Christian (FC) College after Gandhiji's call to quit all British government posts. He had helped build Sikh National College, Lahore, and was its Principal till Pakistan became a reality. It was built to infuse amongst students a sense of fraternity, eradicate the spectre of communal divide, and inculcate in them a sense of national pride in working for an independent, undivided India. Sikh National College was the first college in India, my mother proudly informed me, to fly the *tiranga* flag.

The month flew by. 'Not quite routine' was restored and the Principal Sahib's grandchildren and their friends had worked out many new games to play. Cops and robbers became representative of the British and the Freedom Fighters and, with many permutations and combinations, we never tired of it. Six months after they had left, with our lives forever altered by glimpses of the wider world beyond, my father solemnly informed us that we were moving to Delhi. For once even my pompous elder brother had nothing to say, except to ask 'What does that mean?' It meant we would be living, studying, making new friends, living with my grandparents, and probably not returning to Jamshedpur for a long time. We were grief-stricken, bewildered, and looked questioningly at our mother, only to see her in tears: a first for us. That day, that decision, that move 'for the better' was when the wider tapestry of our lives began unravelling. My father had been invited to join the National Building Organization, a semi-autonomous

Magic show at my birthday party (my mother is expecting Moni), Jamshedpur, 1952.

agency of the Government of India. He was finally going to take up a job linked to his professional qualifications: education and training.

The move to Jamshedpur had been for him a 'no choice' decision. Shanti Swarup Bhatnager, the architect of the 12 institutions of excellence (of which the better known ones still remain the Council of Science and Industrial Infrastructure and Policies (Delhi), National Physical Laboratory (Delhi), National Metallurgical Laboratory (Jamshedpur), Central Food Processing and Technological Institute (Mysore), National Chemical Laboratory (Pune), and Central Fuel Institute (Dhanbad)), was visiting my grandfather in their new house in East Patel Nagar. There he met my father who had returned to an independent India after completing his studies in America and was looking for a job. For some odd reason, on hearing my father was a qualified ceramics engineer, he ordered him to immediately join the German director of the Metallurgical Laboratory in Jamshedpur. Much as my grandparents were distressed to see their son leave once more for a distant place, they decided that the country needed him, an Indian, to assist the German consultant to help steer the institute.

With mild protests on my father's part, that he did not have the requisite qualifications for the job, his future was decided. His was a time when parental permission and decision applied universally across one's destiny in life. He was needed for the task of nation-building in Jamshedpur and that is where he must go. Fortunately for him, he acquitted himself admirably during his tenure there.

- 2 -

Dislocation and Fresh Moorings

The next six months are a bag of jumbled memories. A veil of sadness enshrouded us, the servants not helping by dissolving into tears without any obvious provocation. My most beloved Amma, who was by then on her fourth husband (totally accepted in the Santhali way of life) was not coming with us. Jaggu, the cook's nephew, who had learnt to cook well, came. My only small ray of light was that Farida was already in Delhi with her parents. They had indeed left six months before we did. My mother's distress was palpable because she knew the new job was just part of the story: the 'dutiful loving son' was also going back to be with his parents. She was aware that living with my grandmother was going to be very difficult. As the old proverb goes, two swords cannot fit in one scabbard. My elder brother was equally unsettled, constantly being reminded of the first sundering of his security, the forced move from Lahore to Delhi, and this for him was a second Partition, as he never tired of reminding us. In hindsight, saying goodbye at age 13 to his first 'true love', Mary Jane, must have been factored in.

The pang of watching strangers buying our furniture and accepting that the pigeon and chicken coop would have to be gifted to friends. The the broken promise that I would get *mor pankhi kabutar*s (peacock-tail pigeons) in Delhi did little to assuage my grief. My precious pigeons would fly home to a particular call from me. In hindsight, it was fortunate that our dog Moto had died two months prior to the upheaval. Home became just a house. Seeing my mother work with the *mali* in her precious garden right up to an hour before we left for the station, insisting that it was important to leave the house and garden 'spick and span' for the new occupants, was too much for my younger brother and me. We decided that our father was not really our own but a just a stepfather. It had been my mother's first independent home.

Tearful goodbyes, promises to meet soon. Everyone we knew had come to see us off at the station. Many came with parcels of food, *surahi*s filled with water. It was that special warmth and the sense of belonging to a larger community that is only prevalent in small towns. Train journeys were symbiotic, with many packages of food, in addition to that provided by the railway kitchen (excellent fare in days gone by) and *surahi*s of water. These long-necked earthen pitchers encapsulated fond memories, symbolic of 'being taken care of' before a journey. Many years later, on my first independent train journey, with no one to see me off and say goodbye with the expected *surahi of water* left me heartbroken.

Stepping into our large First Class family compartment was another shock, as its entire length had been packed with plants and cuttings: a miniature garden welcomed us. It had been a conspiracy between the *mali* and mother. My father kept his counsel. This was my third train journey, the first for my younger brother, and for my elder brother the third ride into 'new beginnings'. Like all children, the distraction of being on a train, being waited on by railway attendants at every station, and experiencing all the novelty of a changing landscape, and hearing Hindi being spoken in a variety of unfamiliar dialects soon restored our inquisitive sprits. We spent our waking hours either playing board games or gazing out of the windows and getting our faces powdered with soot. Steam-engines, no air-conditioned compartments, but we did have a private bathroom and toilet. It was a 48 hour journey. At all the larger stations we stepped out of the train and hurriedly walked the length of the platform a couple of times, fearing the train would leave without us.

My parents could only converse about the abject poverty they saw at all the stations: tiny dilapidated shanties at the edge of railway tracks, the deceptive green fields of Bengal and Uttar Pradesh 'which fed the rich but starved the poor'. For once they were in agreement that this was not their vision of an independent India. They had been very active in the student movement in Lahore, enlisting students to join Gandhiji's call for freedom, organizing and attending meetings. We often heard them conversing about the Coffee House in Lahore where they would meet with many other committed student freedom fighters apart from their own inner circle, including Tahira and Manzar Ali. Many years later, Tariq Ali in London gave me his mother Tahira's All India Women's Congress badge. I felt honoured. Young passionate voices in those days were cautioned to speak softly as the British and their fawning Indian supporters had their informers in just such places. They wore khadi as students and my mother got married in a khadi *salwar-kameez,* the only colour provided by the traditional bridal *phulkari* usually embroidered on khadi woven in a pit loom. Friends left behind, a book of poems written by a friend as a wedding present, with a cloth cover which in all probability he had himself stitched, books and photographs were treasures which had perforce to be abandoned, greatly upsetting my parents. We had heard the deep distress in their voices when they spoke of their student years in Lahore and an equal intensity of pain and loss was echoed that day in the train. We realized that my parents were speaking to each other in hushed tones but at the same time felt reassured that their shared grief seemed to bring them closer.

We were required to wash our hands, faces, and necks frequently during the train journey, and bathe on both days. After many minor quarrels and a few fisticuffs over board games, general knowledge quizzes, the unfamiliar but delicious foods Jaggu bought for us at the many stations, our train eventually trundled into Old Delhi Station.

The first strong emotional wave that engulfed my younger brother and me was one of fear. Fearful of the crowds of people, fearful of scrawny barefoot men in red jackets with just a scanty dhotis wrapped around their lower bodies scrabbling and fighting for our luggage, fearful of this strange language being spoken which my mother said was also Hindi. We were afraid too of the loud voices that we mistook to be a universal expression of anger, but were told once more that this was the way people here spoke. We were hurriedly bundled into one of the cars waiting to take us to my grandparents. My father remained behind with two of his new office staff to supervise and bring home the rest of the luggage and of course the many potted plants.

Safely ensconced in the car, where no one was jostling us, we relaxed sufficiently to pay attention to my mother who had assumed the role of a tourist guide. Red Fort, Chandni Chowk, Gurudwara Sis Ganj (so named because the head of the ninth guru Teg Bahadur, beheaded at the orders of Emperor Aurangzeb on 11 November 1675 aged 54, was smuggled here by his followers). My younger brother immediately wanted to know what happened to the head, but my mother was unable to provide a satisfactory answer. Then Gurudwara Rakab Ganj was pointed out where the same guru's body was brought by his devotees. We watched our mother with ghoulish eyes, conspiratorially holding each other's hands and agreeing that Delhi did indeed have many mysterious places to discover. The name Aurangzeb Road stirred memories of my being dragged by my brother from Farida's house and he, after a stern scolding, immediately retracting and accepting that he was a good king. Fortunately for my mother, other distractions did not require much explanation. Parliament House loomed large and then Rashtrapati Bhavan, Teen Murti where Pandit Nehru, our prime minister, lived, North Avenue, South Avenue. We were finally at peace because the traffic was non-existent and the roads more closely resembled those in Jamshedpur. Then Birla Mandir, the crowded roads of Karol Bagh, and finally Patel Nagar.

Basant Kaur, my paternal grandmother, had been given the option of a plot of land in what is now a very posh area of New Delhi which, according to her, was then a 'deserted, isolated jungle which had yet to be developed', or Patel Nagar. She chose the latter, a predictable choice for a refugee as the need to live in close proximity to many familiar faces from Kingsway Camp outweighed any other considerations.

My grandparents were waiting at the gate of their house. They had generously allotted the first floor apartment to us and were waiting for us to lunch together. We sat down at the table and looked at food which was as unfamiliar and uninviting as the other first impressions of Delhi. My grandmother had cooked almost all my father's favourite dishes. Vegetables we had never seen before: *tinda*, *tori* with *channa-dal*, turnips, and some other unpleasant sounding and tasting stuff. The sight of the stuffed *tinda* caused my elder brother to laugh and look at me and say: 'You are one, your nose looks like a *tinda*.' From that day, for the rest of my schooldays I was mercilessly called Tinda: how I hated him; he seemed to be morphing into another being under the very loving eyes of his grandparents. My younger brother, like other minority communities, be it Parsi, or Christian ..., or in this case the youngest child, aligned himself with the majority.

For the next six months all my younger brother and I could keep repeating was 'What are they saying? We cannot understand them.' We tried hard to 'fit in', even in the matter of food which very often gave us stomach-aches, till my mother insisted we get our daily fix of *dal-bhat*. I opted for green beans and Moni for *bhindi,* and that is all we ate for lunch for an entire year. Over the weekend my big treat was *panto-bhat*. Dinner remained familiar: the very same Anglo- Indian menu we had in Jamshedpur.

Culture, language, food, people ... a total breakdown of the 'routine' just transformed something in my nine-year old life. My younger brother reacted by being defiant between intermittent bouts of asthma. My elder brother was admitted to Delhi Public School and within weeks seemed to love it. We younger two were admitted to nearby Springdales School. I was extremely intimidated by the teacher who spoke only in English and looked sternly at me, and who herself could not understand a word I said. She was not at all sympathetic to my mother's explanation that we had just come from Jamshedpur and that Maithili was our mother tongue. Mother might as well have told her we were Martians. Madam teacher's (as that of most people, including our relatives) first reaction to hearing 'Bihar' was, 'You mean *bhuka nanga* Biharis?' My mother's temper, always on a short leash, snapped and she launched into a short crisp history of Bihar, Bihari participation in the freedom movement, and cited many famous freedom fighters from there, some among them now ministers. It required all the tact and diplomacy the principal could muster to get everyone on the same page, while Moni and I, bathed in tears, cowered behind my mother.

I was asked to spell 'night', but my hazy mind could not get it right and I was demoted to a junior class notwithstanding the excellent report and recommendations I carried. Moni fared better, being less intimidated, and was admitted to his designated class. School continued to be a nightmare, replete with many biases and bullying, and so very different from that we had attended in Jamshedpur. I overheard my mother discussing the school's reaction to Bihar with 'Principal Sahib'. If I remember correctly, his reply shocked my mother as his explanation was that most of the children were grandchildren of semi-literate refugees from Partition or children of traders: both these groups were quite uneducated, full of biases, and intolerant of the 'changelings' of Indians from other states and regions. The unfortunate need to cling to a narrow,

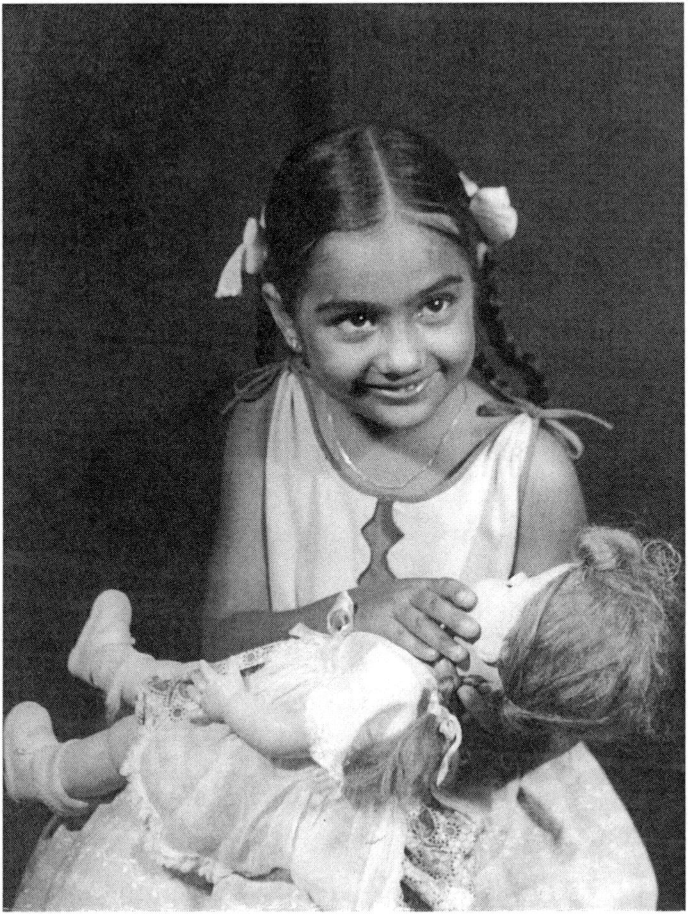

The doll which served as a bribe and won me a friend, Jamshedpur, 1956.

parochial identity had been osmotically transferred to their children. He looked at my mother and said, 'You are Bachelor of Education. These are challenging times; get to work. What cannot be put right immediately is one day going to tear asunder the very fabric of our Constitution and country.' Many years later, after my mother admitted defeat, she reminded us of what our grandfather, the true educationist, had said about eradicating the spectre of the communal divide and inculcating instead a sense of unity and national pride.

I had no friends apart from the milkman's daughter who would accompany her father to deliver milk, and was persuaded to stay and play with me. Perhaps it was the awe of playing with my walky-talky doll that silenced her questions on how I spoke, and so on, and she was ever loyal to me. My identification with her was so deep that the innate need to belong meant that I wanted to dress like her. I was so proud of my new clothes, even of the lice in my hair, because she had them. In Delhi I was overwhelmed by our umpteen cousins, aunts, and grand-aunts, all of whom spoke *potuhari* Punjabi. My mother's relatives spoke a strong *majha jati* Punjabi, while the Punjabis in Delhi had a different dialect. They could however all understand each other notwithstanding a few uncommon words, unlike us Biharis. Every evening we sat with Papaji, my grandfather, who encouraged us to talk about how we were doing in school, our experiences and impressions. He laughed heartily at all our negative reactions, rounding off the conversation with 'Protected frogs from small ponds feel the same when put in a much larger pond with other unfamiliar cousins. Accept the challenges and hold your heads high.' As the principal of Camp College, Karol Bagh, instituted to accommodate the traumatized refugee students who were unable to get admission into Delhi University, his mission was to instil the same principles of harmony, tolerance, and respect for different religions, cultures, food habits, unity, an overriding commitment to work hard for our new country as he had in Sikh National College, Lahore. Traumatized minds however refused to let go of memories and the horror of those last five days when the country turned crimson and was cleaved forever. The young traumatized students could not relate to their Principal's doctrine of forgiveness and unity, leaving him with no other option than to resign. The new Constitution of the Republic of India, he believed, was the only document that should govern our lives and ways. He wanted to make it a compulsory part of the school and college syllabus. In this his view was supported by many other academics, including Maulana Azad, our first Education Minister, but it was never incorporated as a compulsory text in any syllabus except as a special subject in law schools.

On weekends, early morning walks with him from the house to the gardens of Pusa Institute were inspirational. During these he unfailingly reminded us, couched in different amusing anecdotes, that 'We were the pillars of tomorrow's India'. Throughout the week he would have a stream of visitors in the evenings: politicians, professors, his colleagues from Lahore days, old students of FC College and Sikh National College, Khalsa College, Amritsar. All were welcome. They came to seek his advice on a vast range of subjects and would bring their children to receive his blessings. He was in this way a *gurudev* to a large number of people who were still bewildered, trying their utmost to find their feet in the new India. Everyone was greeted with the same warmth and a cup of tea, which was more milk than water.

He had rejected all offers of an official post in the

government, preferring instead to help those institutes which he felt required his expertise His standard answer to all offers was that he had not fought for freedom and gone several times to jail for opportunistic reasons. For him no freedom fighters' pension or the Tamara Patra: The very sound of this award was so comic that it was incorporated in our list of peculiar words and became part of our vocabulary to denote anything outlandish.

From a tight nuclear family we were soon drowning in an extended joint family apart from my daunting list of blood relatives. These included the Baggai family who had moved from Sind. Mrs Baggai, the kindest of people, endeared herself to all of us. She fed us delicious Sindhi tidbits. Our favourite was her walnut and sprouted wheat *barfi*, and I still crave for that unique flavour. They were extending their house by adding two additional floors. Our most exciting game was to jump from our first floor window on to the mound of sand dumped near our gate for construction purposes. The thrill of that jump, fear slowly creeping in: 'What if we don't fall on the sandhill'? kept our adrenalin pumped to the limit. Many years later, reading about the White Russians' penchant for playing Russian Roulette, I was reminded of young limbs suspended between the sky and earth for a split second. That sport continued till a fateful day when Moni did not quite make it and broke his arm. Game over. Moni was the hero of the month, and never tired of proudly announcing to the world at large that his was a multiple fracture.

Then we were introduced to my father's elder half brother, Satwant: the communist. The same communist who had been given leave from jail on my grandfather's surety to attend my parents' wedding. He had absconded to Lucknow instead, where many of his comrades had found supporters and gone 'underground' (another word added to our fast growing vocabulary). My grandfather never forgave him for dishonouring him with the British jail authorities: 'There is honour between adversaries too,' he said. He declared my uncle Satwant persona non grata in the principal's house of Sikh National College, although it was Satwant who had forced my grandparents, mother, brother, and aunts into one of the last trains from Lahore to Amritsar (panic colours the mind with a strange palette). My grandfather had packed his most precious books and papers, my mother just two extra pairs of clothes for my brother and herself.

In panic my grandmother hid the family jewellery in an old potato basket so that no one would snatch it. It was a clever ploy, but alas as this was not confided to my uncle, and he, in his wisdom, failing to understand why she was carrying potatoes, left the basket on the platform. She did however bring with her (primarily to enable her precious grandson to drink water from their own well), a heavy gunmetal *(chist) surahi* with enamel-work and a brass neck made in Qadiyan, which is still in my possession.

We who had grown up with the fervour of an 'imminent Revolution', immediately fell in love at first sight with Satwant Singh, the hero of whom we had dreamt. For us, he was all Three Musketeers rolled into one. He would arrive with three '8 anna' Cadbury chocolates, the largest size then made, one each for the three of us, a practice he continued till we went to college. A standard joke between us and him was that the size of the chocolate determined his financial status. We hung on his every word, only half comprehending what he said. The house was charged with political conversation whenever he came to stay, never for more than two or three days at a time. He carried with him all his worldly belongings in a small attaché case. Three pairs of white khadi kurta-pyjamas, his undergarments, and three khadi turbans, his diary, a few books, depending upon what he was reading, and his toilet bag. He received a stipend from the Party, and this was sufficient for him. I still clearly remember my mother questioning his reading Veer Savarkar's treatise on nationalism. He just laughed and said that he made for very interesting reading. We sat enthralled while he patiently recounted one more 'real life' story. He told us about S. Daya Singh, a comrade who had been arrested by the British in Afghanistan during the Second World War. They had tortured him to extract the name of his associates by dribbling a single drop of water on his head at regular intervals, or worse still, tying a bag full of tiny roaches to his stomach. They never succeeded in getting anything out of him. Many years later I met S. Daya Singh and his gentle wife and was unable to understand how he was not bitter or hated the British. His wife told us that after he was released from jail and sent back to India it took him two years to speak more than a sentence at a time. We also loved hearing Satwant *tayaji*'s 'disguise' stories. How, in independent India, in order to evade arrest, he and his comrades were compelled to disguise themselves. So effective was their disguise that on one occasion, when waiting at a bus stop, my aunt and grandmother walked past him without a trace of recognition. This was all far more exciting than any Agatha Christie books my elder brother loved reading, and when in a good mood would recount to us.

On the opposite side of the pendulum was my father's younger brother Devender *chachaji*, the black sheep of the family who, as a building contractor, was not regarded as being in any 'respectable' profession. His visits from Gwalior heralded much noise, laughter, afternoon sessions of playing Court Piece. There were also regular visits to Wengers or Standard restaurants in Connaught Place for pineapple pastry, chicken sandwiches, and *shami* kababs. We would be ensconced in his 'big' car, a second-hand Buick. It was a car with a mind of its own, especially when 'forced' to climb uphill. My *chachaji's* relationship with his car was, we were told, similar to that which he had with their beautiful mare tethered to the buggy in Lahore. He loved the car, personally cleaned her, and was equally expletive in scolding her for recalcitrant behaviour.

Following page double-spread: Connaught Place, 1950s. (Courtesy: Press Information Bureau).

GLAMOUR
IVORY PALACE
IVORY MART

TESLA
Metz
COSSOR
RADIO
ndo British
GUPTA SPORTS
BOOT
GUPTA
SPORTS

Those were the days of free-range chickens (broiler chickens were introduced in the mid-1970s). I remember my grand-aunt excitedly describing the size of this 'new chicken'. Her son in Punjab bred them at a time when chicken farming was, after the green revolution, the most lucrative business in the agro-Punjab region. My grandmother was however not in the least impressed by what she considered a ridiculous, innovative source of income. She promptly banned broiler chicken from her kitchen: 'The flesh is "phoka" and it has no nutritional value, fed on waste and artificial feeds. Non-fertilized eggs? Nothing could be more vulgar. You are what you eat.'

We loved our cousins who came to Delhi with their eunuch ayah: evidence of another strange belief my *chacha* and *chachi* justified. They felt she was loyal, trustworthy, strong, and their children were safe with her. This was especially so because their experience with the previous care-keeper had not been pleasant (she would mix a dash of opium powder in their milk to keep them quiet). They were regarded as exemplary children at a family wedding, the rest of us horrible rowdy devils, till the truth was discovered. We later heard that this was not an uncommon practice. We also loved it when *chachaji*, as a special treat after dinner when my grandfather had retired to his bedroom, would request her to dance. Joyous, strange, exciting; we had never seen anyone dance like that.

My cousins, Mithu, Shelley, Kaka, and me at my grandparents' in Patel Nagar, 1957.

- 3 -

Family, Amritsar, and New Awakenings

My father would often tell us that 'Sikhs are 2 per cent of the population and 30 per cent of the trouble'. My elder brother wore that statement as a badge of honour, unaware of its implications till many years later. He reminded us that our great uncle was none other than Master Tara Singh, the erstwhile leader of the Sikhs during the Independence negotiations with the British and many years following Partition. There were stories about political intrigues discussed in the Lahore family compound as both sides of the intended divide met to persuade 'Masterji' to 'sign up'. Jinnah maintained that the Sikhs would never be able to live in peace with the Hindu majority; that Islam and Sikhism were both religions of the 'book'. He emphasized that

Sikhism was created to blend together the two major religions, as Guru Nanak was neither a believer in the strict dogma preached by Islam nor an admirer of the idolatry-driven philosophy of Hinduism. Nehru, on the contrary, singled out Mughal rule under which the newly born Sikh community underwent great suffering. The entombment of Guru Gobind Singh's sons because they steadfastly refused to embrace Islam was the constant whisper and the creation of the 'Khalsa', as Guru Gobind Singh and his guerrilla band fought a continuing war with the Mughals. In the end, the Sikhs embraced the Indian Union. Promises were made but history has a long record of disappointments and the repercussions, without passing judgement, reverberated for decades.

Suddenly one day, without any prior notice, I was introduced to Papaji's elder brother and his wife: Maji and Pitaji. He was much shorter than Papaji, dressed in a crisp white khadi kurta-pyjama and a royal blue turban, the exact colour of his eyes. We had never seen an Indian with blue eyes and kept staring at him, which made him laugh as he asked us to come and sit with him. Maji was beautiful, with shiny translucent skin, gentle, loving, also clad in a white khadi *salwar-kameez dupatta*.

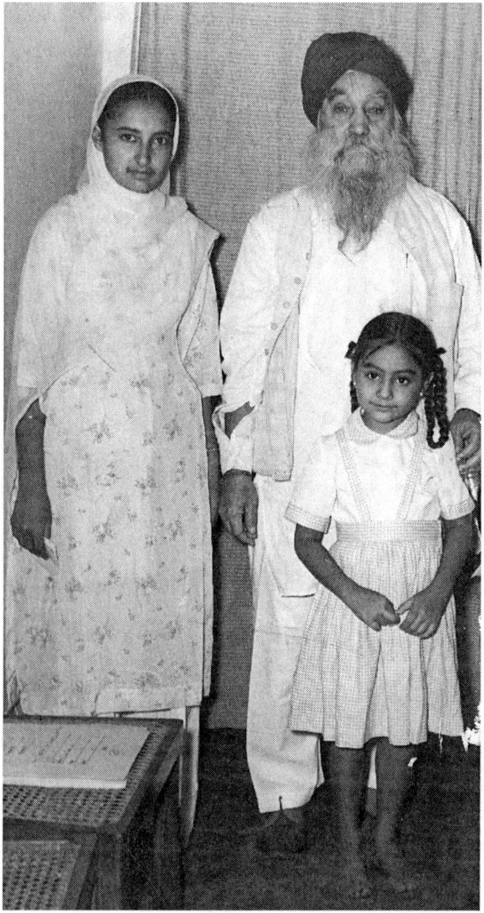

Master Tara Singh, his daughter Dr Rajinder Kaur, and me, 1957.

I instinctively felt safe and comfortable with them.

He had recently been released from jail, his third arrest in independent India. He was perceived as an agent of disharmony in Punjab. All he and the Akali party were demanding was a linguistic plebiscite to protect the Sikh identity from being smothered by the dominant Hindu majority. He had never wavered from demanding that Punjab be declared a Punjabi *suba*, a Sikh linguistic state within India, and a regional 'home' for the Sikhs where the medium of education and the affairs of the secretariat would be in Gurumukhi. A state where Sikhs would be able to honour their heroes, ranging from Maharaja Ranjit Singh to the stalwarts of the freedom movement, stalwarts ranging from Bhagat Singh and his companions to Udham Singh, to the history of Sikhs who had fought for justice for all and protected the weak. To Master Tara Singh and others of the Akali Party, whose unwavering position succeeded in getting parts of Gurdaspur, which was being awarded to Pakistan, officially declared to be part of Indian Punjab. Had that not happened, we in India today would have had no direct access to Kashmir. He argued with passionate clarity that children of Punjab, and especially

Sikh students, should be taught about Punjabi heroes. He was convinced that in the normal course of history they would become postscripts to Jawaharlal Nehru and those he favoured which would pose a serious threat to the future health of the nation. Every state and region in India needed to have regional icons as a source of inspiration for their children. To diminish the contribution of regional leaders in the struggle for Independence in favour of the great pan-Indian leaders would ultimately fail the future generations of children by denying them access to their legitimate 'local heroes'. He was equally passionate about upholding the rights of tribals and the other Indian minorities, insistent that they be recognized as independent of the core Hindu Personal Law and constitutional statutes should acknowledge their uniquness. This was a battle that Ambedkar and others of the same persuasion had lost to the chauvinism of Brahminic orthodoxy.

These convictions were further strengthened when the first census to determine the different languages spoken in India was held in Punjab in the early 1950s. The majority of Punjabi Hindus (egged on by diehard Arya Samajis) when questioned on what their mother tongue was, claimed in Punjabi that their mother tongue was Hindi. Besides, Dalit converts to Islam or Sikhism were not provided 'reservation', and therefore Punjabis from the minority religions converting en masse to Hinduism through the Arya Samaj Shudhi programme, thereby giving Hindus in Punjab a large majority.

Pitaji had come to see his youngest brother and my father, his favourite nephew. I could hear Maji softly telling my grandmother, while I sat close to her, that Pratap Singh Kairon had once more sold the larger interest of the Panth for personal gain. We were speechless. How could it be that in independent India freedom fighters were jailed just because they did not speak the language of the majority? We questioned my father later in the evening: didn't that happen during the British Raj, why is it happening now? A deep sense of injustice, beyond accusing mother of playing favourites, overwhelmed all three of us. Pratap Singh Kairon was at that moment etched in the mind of a nine year old as the greatest villain. I was already reeling under a cloud of 'Not Fair' moments. The move from Jamshedpur, perceived and imagined hostility in school, a butt of constant bullying by my brothers, tiptoeing around my parents' bouts of shadow-boxing. Now I could hang all these life's smaller grievances on a much larger peg: Pratap Singh Kairon, who went around arresting and playing dirty politics with my cherished, newly-discovered, very kind relatives.

I finally met the 'villain' of the piece when he visited my grandparents, which I was told he did quite regularly on his official visits to Delhi to meet the prime minister and other bigwigs in the cabinet. We were horrified that he was welcomed into the house and seemed to be very friendly with my grandparents. Much later in life I realized that many of his visits were to persuade my grandfather to influence his brother, Master Tara Singh, to be more flexible and to merge the Akali Dal with the Congress to fight the Jan Sangh. A number of Akalis with personal ambitions and an eye on political/government posts had already switched loyalties. Fortunately, Papaji was not to be swayed and just laughed off his request, gently reminding Kairon that 'no one in the family was a career politician.'

The most positive fallout of Pitaji and Maji's visit was a letter requesting my mother to let me spend my winter holidays with them. I saw that as my great escape from all that lay at the root of my unhappiness and begged my mother to let me go. That first visit to their very simple house in Ranjitpura in Amritsar changed my life. As neither of his sons had children, I was dearly loved and spoilt, a novelty in an otherwise very formal household. I used to trail my young, brave, spirited, and determined *bua*, Dr Rajinder Kaur, who acted as Pitaji's 'acting personal secretary'. There was a constant flow of people, the sound of typing, occasional bursts of raucus laughter. The three women of the house shared all the housework, and this included milking the cows and buffaloes. Everyone, including Pitaji, washed their own clothes and plates. I was immediately given my roster of tasks: helping to plan the menu for the day bearing in mind everyone's individual preferences. It was a vegetarian household where no one forced me to eat anything that did not appeal to me. Language barriers did not distress or deter me. On one occasion, when asked to fetch the *ganda* from the storeroom, rather than freezing with apprehension, I walked to the room and found to my astonishment that it was *pyaz* that was being sought. Similarly, it was *batau* for brinjals, not *baigan* . . . I wish I could remember more. My most important task was to ensure that Pitaji rested for an hour every afternoon.

I discovered what it meant to be a Sikh: an important lesson that has remained with me. Sikhs fought for justice and always protected the underprivileged from the tyranny of exploitation. Sikhs did not lie; did not think of bettering their prospects at the expense of others. Many years later, when studying Western philosophy, Jeremy Bentham's ideal of the 'greatest good of the greatest number' found resonance in this turning point in my life. Sikhs did not fear adversaries, were self-reliant, and considered no work to be below their dignity. Yes, I visited Harminder Sahib twice a day and helped with all the various voluntary tasks that were performed by devotees. These included cleaning utensils, sweeping, accepting shoes behind the counter, carrying bricks for the construction of an additional wing of the complex. Also, most importantly, going into the *sarovar* with Pitaji and Sant Fateh Singh and helping to clean it. They did not stop me from doing anything I wished. From all this, the fundamental lesson I carried back to Delhi was that you cannot be a Sikh if you are intolerant of other faiths and people.

Meanwhile, my family in Delhi was very uncomfortable with my insistent desire to permanently stay on in Amritsar, my new-found vegetarianism and, above all, my having become a Junior Akali. 'Homecoming' was therefore traumatic, especially at a time when my mother was staging a 'silent mutiny', sometime not so silent, to move out of East Patel Nagar. We could sense the tension between my parents, and especially between my mother and grandmother. I clearly remember the 'day of reckoning', a phrase used by my elder brother to describe that dreadful Sunday. We were getting ready to go to Chandini Chowk for a *khatlama* and *aloo poorie* breakfast followed by juicy *jalebis* fried in pure ghee. I had walked into their bedroom to get the bow on my frock tied (which eventually remained untied that day). There I saw my father looking grim and helpless, my mother packing her clothes and talking to my father in that soft controlled tone she adopted when she was furious. I found it very bewildering to hear her say that even Nora in *A Doll's House* eventually revolted. Who was this Nora and which doll's house? I had been obliged to leave mine behind in Jamshedpur.

I focused on Nora (whoever she was) and refused to believe that I was witness to my mother leaving us. Fortunately, my elder brother enlisted Papaji's help and all was resolved when he uttered just a single sentence. He looked at my father and said 'Every woman must have a house of her own.' That endorsement from his father and our 'restricted' exposure persuaded mine that we should live independently in one of the new government housing colonies and go to 'proper' schools, that is, Moni to St Columba's and I to Carmel Convent. The family moved to a flat on Vinay Marg.

- 4 -

A New Home, New Friends, and New Vistas

Vinay Marg, then known as Diplomatic Enclave, once again re-established for us a familiar lifestyle that had shaped our earliest years in Jamshedpur. The difference was that D1/118, a first floor flat, was smaller than the house we had lived in earlier and rather than a garden there was a huge public lawn in front. The latter was crowded each evening with wannabe cricketers, *pithu* players, cyclists who wanted to become trapeze artists in a circus (indeed, my girlfriend Suneel and I became proficient in all manner of balancing tricks). Older boys and girls pretended to play badminton or cricket but their principal sport was ogling at each other and endeavouring to make eye contact. My brother Surinder naturally glided toward that group.

Moni and I, 1964.

Vinay Marg Revisited, 1987, Neera Batra.

My mother took charge of her own home, with no one any longer looking over her shoulder. Living in a flat was an alien concept and 'flat' was a new term in our vocabulary which we never tired of saying aloud. On our first day in our new home my father proudly expounded to us that this was the new housing concept of modern India and one day, as was already happening in Bombay, Delhi would have huge, high-rising multi-level flats with elevators. Our neighbours, the Belliappas, sent us tea with cakes and sandwiches on the first day, and my mother remarked, 'This is civilized behaviour; you welcome a new neighbour with warmth and kindness.' I could hear her telling the cook to return the tea tray with kababs. Fortunately for my mother, the Belliappas were from Coorg and ate meat with great gusto; we later learnt that their obsession with wild boar was similar to that of the Gauls in *Asterix* comics. Our neighbours on the ground floor were however the Ramaswamys and they, as strict vegetarians, did not eat meat or eggs.

Within a week our hitherto constricted life, where we knew few people, and that too only from Bihar, Punjab, Bengal, Assam, and Orissa, was thrown into a swirl of overwhelming confusion. We learnt that all those who came from south of the Vindhyas were not 'Madrasis'. That there were many different states in the country and although Karnataka, Kerala, and Andhra Pradesh were southern states, people from each of these were differently named. That even the so-called 'Madrasis' were not known as such but were Tamils. They might all be eating idli, dosa, and sambar, and that too only for breakfast, but they also ate different foods and not all of them were vegetarians. Their languages were different and the people from each of the southern states resented being referred to as 'Madrasis', just as we resented being lumped as Punjabis. They were wary of Punjabis, especially sardars, who they thought were very belligerent and had limited brains and of course no culture. All this information was gathered by us during playtime on the 'big lawn' and we would enlighten our parents over dinner. This continued to be served at 7.00 p.m. in summer and 6.30 p.m. in winter, much to the amusement of our new friends, who never dined before 8.30 p.m. We were the aliens, but were not now teased mercilessly but welcomed and accepted just the way we were. These were children of bureaucrats and officers from the armed services who, in their young lives of transfers, relocations, new schools from small districts to state capitals, and in the process of making friends, were quite 'sophisticated' in accepting the 'otherness' of new acquaintances. My mother, however, literally bolted from becoming a member of the colony coffee group after her first encounter with the hierarchy of bureaucrats' wives. All junior wives were expected to stand to attention when the senior wife, invariably the last to enter the room, arrived. Mother would not be subjected to such absurdities and instead, fortunately, re-established friendships with several of her college friends and also women members of our large extended family.

We returned to our routine with a few additional permanent add-ons. Every Sunday lunch was at my grandparents', with my mother frequently absenting herself. Although my grandmother made the appropriate noises of missing her we all knew she preferred it to be so. Once we, her grandchildren, realized it was alright for our mother to absent herself we watched fascinated at the power play between these two strong women whom we dearly loved. The lunch menu would alternate (depending upon the number of guests/relatives) to *chaamp* (mutton ribs) pulao or dried morel pulao, *boondi raita*, and *seviyan ki kheer,* and in winter, *gajjar ka halwa* which would take five hours to cook on a slow charcoal *angeethi*. In winter we would have many kinds of stuffed tandoori *paranthas*, including *keema, sarson ka sag, makki ki roti* with lots of white butter. Another winter treat would be *kanji* made with black and red carrots, cauliflower, and turnip pickle. A real favourite was Mrs Baggai's walnut and germinated wheat *barfi*. We were gradually beginning to enjoy Punjabi food although Bihari flavours continued to rule our palates.

Then there were moonlight picnics at India Gate with relatives, family friends, and their children in summer. This was the India Gate of King George V with the monarch still ensconced beneath his *chhatri,* subsequently replaced by the Amar Jawan Jyoti. The ritual began with boating in the adjacent water body on one side of Rajpath. This was followed by a narration of a brief history on the British Raj and the making of New Delhi accompanied by a general knowledge quiz. This was certainly the highlight of the picnic for my father, but for us children it was that one episode that spoilt our fun. All we wanted to do was to scamper around like mad dervishes, cajoling a benevolent adult to buy us balloons and ice creams. The latter invariably led to a debate on the relative merits of Caryhom, Keventer, and Kwality, especially for the wannabe gourmands who would insist on the superiority of the chocolate used in the Keventer chocobar. There would be the, oh so tempting, *channa chor gram walas* and the *lakkar hazam patthar hazam churan walas*, and the most amazing massage-*wala* seducing prospective clients by calling out in a dulcet tone *'tel malish chamki'*. My elder brother once actually got taken in and to this day rues the memory. Then there were the most dangerous peddlars, the ear-cleaners with their deadly instruments. We were threatened with dire consequences if we even approached any one of these 'unsavoury' characters. In winter, the picnic venues would shift to late Sunday mornings in Lodhi Gardens, Qutab Minar, Jamali Kamali (which was then quite unkempt), Tughlaqabad, and Hauz Khas. My father's history lessons would traverse several centuries, ranging from the Slave Dynasty to the Lodhis, Tuglaqs, and Mughals.

My mother had a few fixed ideas about picnic foods, no doubt influenced by her American and German

King George V in regal splendour.

friends from Jamshedpur, so our share of the picnic basket would be a cold chicken roast, Russian salad, egg sandwiches, and kababs. Most of all, however, I loved dipping into my aunt's *khatta channa* and cold *poories*. There were other picnickers but we never felt hemmed in, all of us creating our own private islands, and just hearing one anothers distant voices, everyone having a good time.

No other picnic event was more eagerly awaited than with Agya uncle (Agya Kar Bakshi) and his family. He was my father's first cousin and among the most colourful characters I have ever known. The first story I heard originated from the Lahore days. Fearful that his wastrel ways would doom his education, his parents sent him to live with our family in the familial compound. The argument was that the 'educational aura' of living with his educationist uncle would move him in the right direction.

About every two or three weeks, the three of us would be bundled into the car with dhurries and hampers in the 'dickie' and driven to India Gate to meet up with Agya uncle and his family, two boys and a girl on either side. Four adults and six children with appropriate

Punjabi nicknames — Tutu, Tinu, Moni, Shayrie, Duma, and Chandi — would converge at a prime locale after sundown, stake our claim to a choice corner, and set up house. The mothers would take off for a walk down Rajpath, the fathers would engage in profound discourse centred around politics, and the six samurai would race around like sirens. Soccer, kabaddi, badminton, relay races ... and mayhem followed. Then came the quintessential moment. The short drive to Pandara Road Market for dinner. The expedition was always led by Agya uncle and selected *baccha*s, an honour that was pursued with competitive zeal. I hated the fact that he was solicitously even-handed, a very noble virtue except when it was not your turn. I have vivid memories of what transpired. When we arrived at the dhaba, the chef would promptly abandon his place, which was then occupied by my uncle. He would clasp the *karchi* and stand over the *karahi*, as if poised with his baton, preparing to conduct the New York Philharmonic in a rousing rendition of the *William Tell* Overture. Ah, what a visual orgasm. A pinch of this, a smidgeon of that, a splash of mystery followed by a flaring flame, the wafting aroma of garlic, ginger, and what not. The drive back to India Gate to partake of this gourmet meal was painful as the aroma of the food in the car overpowered our pangs of hunger.

None of these memories would be complete without relating the *magaz* evening. We were gathered once more at the dhaba, watching the maestro conduct. Things were looking good, gastronomic juices were overflowing, and soon we would be enjoying the fruits of his labours. Just as we expected Agya uncle to complete the ritual with a final flourish of his baton, the chef emerged from his hiding place and said, 'Sahib, today we have *magaz*'. The look on my uncle's face was awesome: the holy grail expression. He turned and said, '*Chalo*, bring it'. Off went the chef to the kitchen. Our curiosity could have killed a generation of cats but we all knew better. This was an epochal, subliminal moment not to be interrupted by juvenile interrogation. Soon the plate was uncovered to reveal a sludge of yellow curds. With a glazed look the maestro stepped on to the podium. This was a new movement we had never heard before. It rose up from a hitherto unplumbed depth, gentle in tone while rich in emotional reverberations. Simple in its design, no complexity other than the basics with the addition of *pudina*. The ritual at dinner was different too.

We were not handed plates with food served, but that evening were asked our preferences. I, always the most courageous, was the first to request a dollop of the *magaz* with the question, 'It looks different; what is it?' There was no hesitation in my uncle's response, 'goat brains'. None of the six samurai believed him but five stepped back and only I ventured where none of us had been before. Tasted alright, actually. Makes sense because my culinary proclivities began early. To this day, I truly enjoy spiced *magaz* with a tandoori roti. The drive back to India Gate was surreal; silence ruled.

New Delhi's population was very sparse then in comparison to what it is today, and we could travel from Vinay Marg to Connaught Place in 15 minutes. On many of the arterial roads leading to the centre of town, like Akbar Road, Aurangzeb Road, Curzon Road, King Georges Avenue ... we could even count the number of cars on our fingertips, except during the office rush. I do not remember ever being caught in a traffic jam. That might happen in Bombay and Calcutta but never in New Delhi. A few of the officers living in our crescent of flats, especially the colonel, cycled to office to keep fit and conserve petrol. The roads were a safe haven for cyclists

and pedestrians. There were then no marauding giants driven by spoilt young adults or arrogant chauffeurs taking the cue in bad behaviour from their masters with their newly acquired wealth, and claiming ownership of roads and immunity for their misdeeds.

Connaught Place, 1950s (Courtesy: PTI).

Gymkhana Club replaced Beldih Club, although it took us a while to accept that we were swimming in a pool where till recently 'Dogs and Indians [were] not allowed.' The pool was and still is called Lady Willingdon's Bath, a charming acknowledgement of some of the pleasurable sporting activities to which the British introduced us by default (let's pray that no misguided nationalist fervour leads to changing that name too). We went swimming almost every day, and there were also tennis and squash classes for my brothers. I tried my hand at tennis, but playing at 3 p.m. on a hot summer's day was not my idea of fun. The pool, on the other hand, was a happy, friendly, inviting place and almost everyone knew one another. We played water polo, while water fights erupted spontaneously between the girl and boy gangs, and I am aware of some long-lasting romances having been born there. We gazed with admiration at some of the older boys and girls who all looked so glamorous and hoped that we would soon resemble them. We were allowed a plate of potato chips and a cold Vimto after our swim, and a weekend treat would be a plate of chicken sandwiches, for which I still occasionally crave.

Lady Willingdon Swimming Bath, Gymkhana Club, New Delhi (Courtesy: Tejbir Singh).

The Annual Children's Christmas party at the

LADY WILLINGDON SWIMMING BATH
1936

Gymkhana Club was one of my favourites. We would all sit on the dance floor around the Christmas tree, perhaps 200 to 300 kids, at the feet of a hearty Santa. Then began the roll-call. As names were called, each kid would rise and go to Santa, who would hand over a wrapped package with a hearty 'Ho Ho Ho'. Then the next and the next in succession. All of us completely bought into the myth of a big, fat man attired in a red clothes riding a sleigh drawn by flying reindeer, dropping down chimneys with presents for kids. How on earth was he aware of that special thing that I most wanted for Christmas? When we discovered the 'kiddie fraud', it was a devastating blow. The presents were actually purchased by the parents and given to the club for onward transmission to us.

Soon we had graduated from children's Christmas parties to teenage dances. These were fraught with tension, stress levels rising every day a fortnight before D Day. Reminiscent of Victoriana, the boys would sit or casually lounge on one side of the marvellous spring dance floor in what was called the ballroom and the girls were primly seated on the opposite side, pretending to be engrossed in conversation. Then one young 'man' would muster the courage to walk the breadth of the room and ask his girlfriend for a dance, snapping the suspense and opening up the path for others to follow. The designated chaperones would keep their beady eyes fixed on the dance floor. Why oh why did we find this very excruciating event so exciting? Planning days in advance what to wear, hoping that the most popular and exciting boys would request a dance. Then there was the El Cid year. Those of us in *churidar-kameez* draped our *dupattas* to cover our heads and swinging the ends over our shoulders, imitated Sophia Loren. We jived, rock n' rolled to Elvis Presley and Ricky Nelson, fox-trotted to Pat Boone, Frank Sinatra, and Dean Martin. Some young couples got away sneaking a kiss behind a pillar. This tantalizing event with 'exciting possibilities' concluded at 9.00 p.m.

We three siblings learnt quite early the correlation and intimacy between tears and laughter, making us great trapeze artists balancing the multiple waves of mother's mood swings. We also mastered the fine art of tiptoeing when her dark moods compelled us to move silently around the house, but there was also her sunny, vibrant side, when the world within would suddenly be uplifted, enveloping us in a whirl of beauty, laughter, board games, great mind games, impromptu scripts written and plays performed.

A myriad of the most enticing fragrances wafted from the kitchen, the cook inspired by my mother's tutelage reaching the penultimate of his repertoire. Yet we tiptoed. It was always difficult to discern which was the real world. Then one day my elder brother understood and confided to my brother and me that both worlds, the dark and the bright, were just the flip side of the same coin. 'Coin?' my younger brother asked; 'You mean mama?' To wake up late (another endearing quirk of my mother was to let us sleep as late as we wanted on holidays (not for her the Victorian dogma of the early bird). To wake up late on a Sunday to the bewitching voice of Begum Akhtar meant that we were in for a gastronomic treat: the traditional family Sunday Brunch.

Growing up in Delhi inevitably meant learning to deal with the searing summers. Delhi houses and flats were built of brick and cement, and when the temperatures rose, the interiors would begin to simmer. Fans were of little use because they just re-circulated hot air. The rooftop, open-air option worked well until the monsoon arrived. As we lived on the first floor, we claimed the

At the entrance of Grand Hotel, Simla, 1964.

terrace and the *chhath* was laid out every evening like a dormitory with charpoys and *gaddas*. After dinner, we would migrate upstairs to play 'constellation spotting', thrilled to see a falling star. Otherwise we would just gaze over the parapet and count fireflies flitting in and out of the hedges. It was magical. During the days, desert coolers performed an admirable job, at least cooling the flat until the monsoon arrived when the resulting humidity crippled their usefulness. I recall being in high school before my father acquired our very first air-conditioner, which was dutifully installed in my parents' bedroom. It was a second-hand Carrier purchased at an embassy sale and served us well for several years. When the heat became quite unbearable, we would all bundle into their bedroom to sleep.

As May drifted into June, we would prepare for our annual two-week retreat. Simla was the preferred destination because there my father was given a discounted rate at Grand Hotel, which was then owned by the government. Soon enough, July was upon us and we descended back to Delhi to prepare for another school year. The monsoon always seemed to arrive around the middle of July, close to the day schools and colleges reopened after the holidays.

Yes, indeed, summers were eagerly awaited almost like a masochistic ritual, the heat be damned. Life decelerated with the holidays, traffic eased, Delhiwallahs were too hot and bothered to argue, parents seemed more obliging (at least until report cards landed in the mailbox), lifelong friendships were cemented... I could go on... but those were very special times indeed.

The predictability of our lives, with fresh timetables drawn for every school term, became a cocoon of security which we tenaciously protected. There were picnics, visits to friends, birthday parties, a few children's plays/puppet shows, Roy Rogers and other cowboy and Red Indian Hollywood films in three of the poshest cinema halls (Plaza, Odeon, and Rivoli). We were taken to classical Hindustani music concerts at the Shankar Lal Festival — mercifully the last was short and sweet because, more often than not, it continued well past our bedtime.

The major excitements took place outside our lives, but greatly impacted us. The language issue was not only an emotional one in Punjab but equally so in the southern states. In the late 1950s/early 1960s a few staunch Hindu politicians from north India, driven by their own myopic struggle to survive another election, rabble-roused the Hindi 'cow belt' by raising the spectre of Hindi as the national language. That proved sufficient to ignite flames that spread faster than Hanuman's tail did in Lanka among non-Hindi speaking Indians. These I think were in the majority, if you count too the states of the north-east and the Punjabi and Urdu speaking populations.

Our very liberal prime minister Jawaharlal Nehru's ambition was to lead his country to an inspiring modern industrial future. He envisaged the new temples of India to take the form of dams, industries, bridges, museums, cultural and educational centres, and research institutions manned by brilliant young Indian scholars and technicians returning from prestigious educational institutions in the West. This he believed would ignite the imagination of the Indian people. and they in turn would be motivated to participate in building the new India of his dreams. Many of these ambitious plans were destined to be jettisoned amidst the reality that India was riddled by bigotry and regressive ideologies which were, and remain, a motivating force behind a very large number of Indians who do not think with their heads

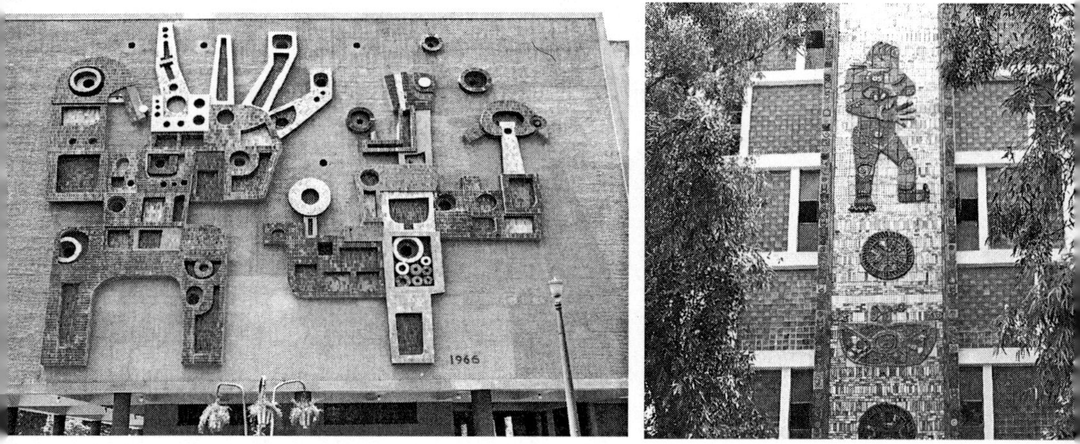

but act through narrow, superstitious hearts. Their understanding of independent India was far removed from the modern, stimulating, and challenging journey envisaged by India's first prime minister. It must have come as a rude shock for him to discover that all Indian leaders of large constituencies did not share his enlightened vision, and that their views were echoed by some of his own cabinet ministers. To discover that regional, religious, caste, and class identities were the dominant discourse.

Views of Satish Gujral's murals on the walls of Shastri Bhawan and Baroda House – Headquarters of Northern Railways, New Delhi, 1966.

My father would bundle us into the car over weekends and point out all the new buildings and those under construction. Sapru House built in the tradition of the Bombay, J.J. School of Architecture; Vigyan Bhavan, the WHO building; Rabindra Bhavan, and a host of others. Art, sculpture, and engineering were combined in the new architecture and for the first time, we saw the use of murals to embellish building façades: Satish Gujral's murals on the walls of the High Court and Shastri Bhavan and many more public buildings in Delhi. Inspired by the socialist murals of Diego Rivera, David Siqueiros, and others in Mexico, and M.F. Husain's mural on the walls of Indraprastha Bhawan.

Our dinner-table conversations would get an added colour when either my Communist uncle (*tayaji*) or my aunt (Rajinder *buaji*) would join us on one of their visits to Delhi. I first heard the name Patrice Emery Lumumba, a strange name indeed, on a hot June evening in 1960. We did not have air-conditioners then and the one giant cooler often rebelled against overuse. We were in no mood to linger over dinner but the excitement in *tayaji*'s voice caught our attention. From earlier conversations we were aware that King Leopold II's so-called Belgian

Congo, whose natural resources had been ravaged by the Belgians, had finally been liberated from its colonial masters. We had just sat down for dinner when *tayaji* came rushing into the room to announce that Patrice Lumumba had been elected the first democratically elected leader of Congo. With great pride (as if he were our leader), *tayaji* told us that Lumumba was determined to utilize the Congo's natural resources to improve the living conditions of his people. Ironically, seven months to the day, when I was reading the current events in the morning Assembly in school, I had to announce Patrice Lumumba's assassination: 'one of the most important assassinations in the twentieth century'. The following ten years would witness many other political assassinations, with America, one of the sponsors of Lumumba's, taking the lead.

Growing up in Vinay Marg provided us with a sense of security similar to that which may have been experienced by the Israelis in their kibbutzim. It was a sense of all of us being members of a single community. Neighbours dropped by for a chat or coffee on weekends, or during their after-dinner walks, without waiting to be invited. We were always in and out of our friends' homes, freely helping ourselves to hot buttered toast with jam or honey. The adults were indulgent yet watchful. Any misdemeanour was immediately reprimanded by whichever adult was present, whether parent or otherwise.

Evenings saw all the children of Vinay Marg out in the playground or cycling around the blocks. Some stayed at home, either playing the piano or practising some form of Indian classical music or dance. We revelled in strolling around the block where Mr Krishnamurthy lived in a ground floor flat, and we could hear the tinkling of Yamini Krishnamurthy's *gunghroo*s accompanied by her sister Jyotishmati singing like an angel.

We went for picnics on our own to the Aravalli Hills, now called Yashwant Place. For us it was a place steeped in mystery and menace with its massive boulders of reddish-coloured rock, deep gullies where the sweetest wild berries grew alongside lantana bushes. Many of our plans to realize our childhood ambitions and fantasies, of what we would do when we turned 18, were plotted here. The most fantastical were entrusted to the secret nooks and crannies of the solid rocks. These, like our dreams, were eventually pulverised to powder, known as Badarpur-gravel, used for construction purposes. We could not believe that the area was going to be 'developed', and before our horrified eyes what was once a magical wilderness, home to many creatures, including jackals, was turning into a horrible concrete and cement monster. The only consolation was that after our earlier very enjoyable visits to the legendary Sheila Cinema hall, near distant New Delhi Railway Station, the new Chanakya Cinema hall arose majestically in our very neighbourhood. Besides, as with Sheila Cinema, it had a 70 mm screen.

There was just one area which was out of bounds for us children. This was sprawling 'slum' where almost all our 'part time' domestic workers lived. It was squalid, and without any basic civic amenities. The people who squatted there were miserably poor, as we were horrified to learn from our cleaning lady who had worn new clothes only on her wedding day. Today, after the passage of over three decades, that slum has developed into what is called Nehru Park, over 80 acres of greenery, where we Vinay Marg *walas* had all assembled on the memorable day when Lenin's statue was installed. It remains probably one of the few places where Lenin still stands upright.

Connaught Place, across Queensway (later changed to Jan Path) as Kingsway had been changed to Raj Path, and Karol Bagh, were the only places to shop, apart from Chandni Chowk, which was for us more a food destination as its other shops remained closed on Sundays. Connaught Place was for us the preferred shopping destination as Karol Bagh was too distant and grossly overcrowded. The shops closed their doors for long lunch breaks which always worked to our advantage as my mother, 'to kill' time, would perforce take us to Wenger's, and there we would gorge ourselves on pineapple pastry or chicken patties. Both items still retain their original flavour and the gentle aura of yesteryear still gracefully cling to these establishments. The only two shops that I know of today that continue to practise this very civilized habit of a long lunch break, regardless of the loss of revenue, are Arora Stores and the chemists in Nizamuddin East Market.

On the occasional Sunday, a group of us, supervised by an adult, would cycle all the way to Shantipath for a sightseeing trip of the embassies and high commissions, and settle down to a hearty picnic on the lawns bordering the avenue. With daredevil swagger, much to the embarrassment of our designated chaperone, on two occasions we even knocked twice at the Prime Minister's gate, impudently asking to see him. To our surprise, on both occasions we struck lucky. The guard went in, and returned smiling, welcoming us in. We had tea with our beloved Chacha Nehru who showed us the private zoo he had created, were served biscuits with tea, and went home to brag.

Our cycling expeditions also took us to V.K. Krishna Menon's house a few times as one of the accompanying 'uncles' knew him. After tea (we were informed by his secretary that Krishna Menon drank at least 30 cups of tea a day) he would quiz us on our general knowledge and advise all the girls in the group to learn Bharatanatyam. We gazed at him with awe as the man who had spoken non-stop for 7 hours 48 minutes in 1957 to the members of the UN Security Council. On that occasion he had defended India's position on Kashmir after the Pakistan foreign minister had opened the debate on Kashmir being declared a part of Pakistan. Krishna Menon, our hero, had collapsed with exhaustion over halfway through his speech and was hospitalized. Undeterred, he returned to complete his speech which continued for another hour with a doctor monitoring his blood pressure. Nothing could have been more romantic, heroic, and moving; pure theatre. This was especially so because after that long and impassioned speech the Soviet Union vetoed the resolution on Pakistan's claim to Kashmir.

The next in line of heroes of the UN for us was, logically, the Soviet premier Nikita Khrushchev, who was incensed at the provocative criticism by the Philippines' representative to the UN Assembly in 1960. The delegate accused the Soviets of a hegemonistic tendency and grave human rights violations in Eastern European countries. Our Hero protested by banging his fists on the table in front of him, and then took off his right shoe — loafer or sandals as he was averse to laced shoes. — and banged it with all his might. The force of it caused objects on the lectern to bounce and the assembled delegates were forced into an eerie silence. The newspapers quoted his comment: 'It was such fun'. We were bowled over.

Our flats faced Safdarjung Airport used by the Indian Air Force for practice sorties. We would see icons of the Second World War, Tiger Moths and Hunters, flying over our colony through the week. Over the weekends we would be fascinated by the gliders gently floating in the sky like giant clouds, yet apparently far more fragile than the clouds. As they flew at a much lower altitude than aeroplanes, we would wave to the pilots and were thrilled when they acknowledged us. Many, many years later the husband of a dear friend died in a gliding accident there, having taken off from the flying club's base; that too was the fate of Sanjay Gandhi, whose small plane, also part of the flying club, crashed in the same area.

In the early 1960s. the large hangar, used as a workshop by Air Force engineers, caught fire. Nothing in any film we had seen had prepared us for such a sight of devastation within minutes of its occurrence. The fire engines had a minor role to play as the building was nearly reduced to cinder by the time they arrived. We had rushed to the roof of our flat to witness flames almost as high as our building spreading their tongues with great ferocity accompanied by the sound of an explosion within the hangar. Fortunately it was during the workers' lunch break so there were no casualties. (I wish I could say the same for the many large and small fires that coloured the skyline of Delhi crimson during the 1984 massacre of the Sikhs.)

- 5 -

Sombre Times and the India-China War

1960 was a strange and exciting year replete with predictable and unpredictable events. The statue of King George V facing India Gate, a tribute to 82,000 soldiers of undivided British India who died during the First World War, was removed from its pedestal. We toppled the king: no act of valour or demonstration of a confident nation. One of the many inexplicable moments of mean-spirited empty gestures that aimed at obliterating landmarks of our history. Years later, sensibly, as an act of homage to the Indian jawans who died in 1971 during the liberation of Bangladesh, a simple structure in black marble was constructed, surmounted with an eternal flame, the Amar Jawan Jyoti, with a reversed rifle capped with a war helmet. Even we, just into our teens, were conscious that bringing down statues and renaming roads were meaningless, symbolic gestures. The subject generated heated arguments at our dining table, and also among our gang of friends, as did the issue of English versus Hindi. The trump card among my peer group was when someone put it in a nutshell: 'If English is not our common language then how will we communicate with one another?' Certainly not in our regional languages and most certainly not in Hindi with our south-of-the-Vindhya friends.

1960 was also a landmark year as Chou En Lai paid a state visit to India. Those were the days of the Hindi-Chini Bhai-Bhai relationship. Our school was one of those chosen to line up their students alongside the road from the airport to Rashtrapati Bhavan. We stood there with tiny Indian and Chinese flags fluttering in our tiny hands shouting 'Hindi-Chini Bhai-Bhai' as the cavalcade drove past with both Jawaharlal Nehru and Chou En Lai waving regally towards us. For us, that was the highlight of his visit.

Snippets of adult conversation, however, indicated that all had not gone as planned. It clearly could not have, as on 20 October 1962 China declared war on India and

Pandit Nehru and his cabinet greeting Chou En Lai and his delegation at the airport, 1960 (Courtesy: PIB).

INDIAN AIR FORC

was in complete ascendance throughout that horrific month till the ceasefire was declared on 20 November. Much changed forever in our young lives because the war made us acutely aware of the brutal reality of border conflicts. All the women were given rough wool to knit socks, pullovers, and caps for our brave soldiers who were ill-equipped and even less prepared to face the heavily armed Chinese soldiers snug in their protective combat uniforms. My mother promptly returned the rough coarse wool provided as she said it cut her hands and would be equally damaging for the jawans. She was determined to do the brave soldiers proud by knitting her quota from the purest wool she could afford. A dozen exquisite socks and caps were handed over to a bemused major who had been sent to collect them and chivalrously thank the ladies in the gallant armed force style. He looked utterly overwhelmed when all the ladies piled his plate high with food as if he were a starving jawan from the front who had come down just for this occasion. My mother's bundle was given place of honour.

Jawaharlal Nehru's sense of betrayal was palpable and a few schools decided that they had to rally around him. Our Mother Superior's inspirational lectures to support our brave jawans and officers by donating our pocket money to the Prime Minister's Relief Fund was accepted in the 'right spirit of patriotism'. Clutching our precious savings in little pouches, we marched from our school which was close to the prime minister's house. Jawaharlal Nehru came down to the reception hall to greet us and we gasped at his appearance: he looked 10 years older than the last photograph we had seen of him. Shaking hands with all of us, he maintained a brave smile and we dropped our pouches in the large donation bag. Adjacent to it was another for donations of gold. My friend was wearing a gold chain which she promptly removed and popped in. She was confident that her parents would not be angry but appreciative of this act. How I enviously wished at that moment that I had been wearing a gold chain, or better still, gold bangles, which I would have slid off my wrist into the waiting bag. Alas, on that occasion I was not intended to be the hero of the day. I do know, however, that all our mothers did donate some of their gold jewellery, and for one of my aunts it was an opportunity to rid herself of most of the ugly things gifted by her mother-in-law.

Almost exactly two years after the ceasefire, when a dear friend of my parents, Colonel Balwant Singh Ahluwalia, returned from a Chinese prison, he told us that they had not received a single pair of woollen socks or pair of warm shoes (they had been fighting in the snow in khaki PT shoes) or anything else. The depressing and recurrent rumour was that they had been hawked in the bazars of Calcutta. It took the Indian army almost a year to obtain a comprehensive list of Indian soldiers and officers who were being held in Chinese prisons. That one year was the most painful in our young lives, as we could literally see Colonel Balwant Singh's wife shrivel up, and his ageing parents cease to smile. We took it upon ourselves as a personal responsibility to play with their two sons and cause them to smile and laugh. It was also the first time I saw my mother, as a true believer of the Sikh faith, go to the gurudwara every morning for 40 days for the Asa di Var, praying for her friend's safe return. Return he did, with many stories of extreme cowardice on the part of some Indian army officers in sharp contrast to the kind and caring treatment all the prisoners of war had received in Chinese prisons. That Colonel Balwant Singh returned alive was thanks to the efficient medical attention given to him by Chinese doctors. He, in later years, withdrew his earlier statement and praised the Indian army and his colleagues, claiming he had ordered them to leave him. (My mother, however, has always maintained that a first information report is invariably the most authentic.)

A terrible fallout of the war was the way Chinese residents in India, who had always lived harmoniously with their Indian neighbours, were treated. My mother told us it was not as grim as the treatment meted out to the American Japanese after the bombing of Pearl Harbour, but all the same disgraceful and shameful. She was particularly vociferous as her Chinese 'shoe artist' was arrested from his shop in Connaught Place under alleged charges of spying. She immediately wrote a letter to the Secretary, Home Affairs, in his defence, affirming his good moral character. The Secretary, a friend of my father's, called him to report what my mother had done and to say that she could be arrested for treason. For our part, we, her children, have often wondered whether for that split second my father might well have wished her a brief term in prison.

The new school term in the 1960s began in January,

a somewhat cold and depressing month, following the rollicking winter vacations which either took us to my mother's village, Sheikhupura near Amritsar, where we connected with our 'rustic and rural' selves, or to the jungles of Dehradun and Rishikesh.

My maternal grandfather (also a member of the Akali Dal) had donated several acres of his land to build a school for the children of many villages in the district and was popularly called Headmaster Sahib. He was determined that his city-bred grandchildren should not lose touch with their rural background and insisted that all the sons of the family go, like most of the villagers, to the fields to answer calls of nature. My girl cousin and I were also put through this regimen till my elder cousin's periods began and much to the relief of all her younger cousins, we never had to 'go rural' again. Many years later, when I was working at Saheli (the women's resource centre) two young Indian women, Yale graduates, spouted their textbook learning of India. I asked them impatiently whether they had ever squatted in the fields to relieve themselves or read the writings of Chaudhury Charan Singh, Madhu Limaye, Ram Manohar Lohia, or Jayaprakash Narayan. If not, I requested that they do so and then return to Saheli and tell me about the 'real' India.

Returning back in time, school in January was also tinged with other bitter-sweet memories. Our school reports were posted to our homes. My brothers never had to worry because they fared consistently well. I, on the other hand, was an erratic student, sometimes among the first five in rank and sometimes among the last two. We had established a pact with our friendly postman to hand over the reports to us personally and to no one else. Yes, those were the days of the postman: long letters painstakingly written in long-hand to friends and relatives, anxiously awaiting their replies, and collecting stamps and postcards. The pink-coloured telegram usually portended bad news and we really dreaded getting one of those. Long-distance telephone calls were a luxury and the excitement of being introduced to new technology — telex messages — resulted in super fast communication across states. We were very proud of our postal service and boasted to all my father's 'foreign' friends that the post never got lost or was delivered to the wrong address. The postman was the real hero, because it was through him that the whole of India remained connected.

Many years later it was through telex messages and telegrams that a few anxious journalists who had been covering elections in Assam warned and beseeched Indira Gandhi, our then prime minster, to urgently send additional troops to the north-eastern part of Assam where the Bodos, with the support of the ULFA, were marching towards the Muslim villages, particularly Nellie. Muslims had dared to vote in the state elections, in the face of ULFA's call to boycott them. In just 24 hours 3,500 children, men, and women were killed. The *Statesman* carried the most horrific photograph taken by Raghu Rai of hundreds of babies and children all laid in rows awaiting burial. A very black morning in an otherwise sunny day in New Delhi. The few grieving relatives who escaped the massacre still await justice. Writing about it so many years later my fingers still become unsteady.

The only silver light at the end of the very bleak tunnel that period presented was the Republic Day Parade on 26 January. Like most parades throughout the world, apart from the celebration in Mexico, 'the Day of the Dead', or the Carnival in Brazil, it was a display of military might leavened by tableaus showcasing the progress or natural beauty of individual states. Children from many schools would also participate, marching proudly down Rajpath saluting our prime minister and marching ahead with great pride. Yes, we were proud to be Indians and this day marked a collective sense of faith in our country and its achievements, however we might differ from each other through the rest of the year. On 26 January we showcased to the rest of the world and to one another our unity in diversity. A week earlier our excitement would reach a hysterical pitch, and there was no other subject of discussion either in school or at the large playground except about attending the parade. This would be followed by planning a picnic menu suitable for this solemn celebration. A large basket would be packed with boiled eggs, chicken or ham sandwiches, apples, oranges, and a fruit cake. We were discouraged from drinking anything, except rationed sips of water as the toilets set up for the day were at a distance.

A month prior to the parade we would watch with eager anticipation as the PWD staff erected the green benches, labelling each segment A, B, C ... all along Rajpath, from India Gate to Vijay Chowk, indicative of where we would be seated. When the day arrrived we were awoken at the crack of dawn as we all had to be in our seats by 7.30 a.m. No one grumbled about getting up early. My mother's only concern was whether we had 'gone' or not: never before or after have I seen my mother so preoccupied with her children's bowel movements. The children all sat on durries right in front, and the section adjoining us was reserved for the prime minister and all the other dignitaries with the members of the press suspended in a box above them. The chief guest, a visiting prime minister, president, king or queen, accompanied our President in an open Victoria carriage drawn by six horses trotting smartly with the President's Bodyguard as outriders. We were in a frenzy of excitement, which abated for just a few moments when one too many platoons marched by, but then came the flypast which would once again raise the level of hysteria. We ate almost non-stop throughout the parade, sharing food with our new-found friends. This frenzy of consumption was interrupted only for an hour before the flypast in order to avoid attracting predatory kites who would pose a serious threat to the air force pilots. It was a jolly, carefree atmosphere with a strong sense of comraderie among all who were present. There were no security men with machine guns, no frisking by security personnel, no barriers or police check-posts. Some of us would for a brief moment sneak into the VIP segment just for the fleeting opportunity to sit with our leaders.

The 1963 Republic Day parade was particularly poignant as it was just after the life-changing war with China. There was a moment in time when the cabinet debated, as did editors in the Op Ed pages, whether it was appropriate to hold the parade at all, but in the true tradition of 'the show must go on' the cabinet gave the go-ahead. With the loss of thousands of army personnel and a major number of platoons still stationed close to the border, Nehru decided that civil organizations would also be invited to march, especially those that had voluntarily contributed to the war effort.

The largest contingent in this category to be invited by him were the *swayamsevaks* of the RSS, 3,500 of them marching in full uniform, khaki shorts and white shirts, accompanied by their band, smartly saluting our prime minister. To all the criticism from within his cabinet and the Congress party, as also many academicians and journalists, Nehru justified this by saying that 'the members of the RSS were also Indians and had worked tirelessly to alleviate the suffering of our jawans'. (The adults in my family concurred with his rationale.) At the Beating Retreat, the culmination of the Republic Day celebrations, when a combined band of the three armed services began playing 'Abide With Me', Gandhi's favourite hymn and the traditional finale to the ceremony, there was not a single dry eye among the public, all of whom had come to honour the brave soldiers and officers who had laid down their lives in a senseless war.

Many years later the RSS cadre were also the first to reach coastal Andhra, even before the army did. There, after a devastating cyclone, thousands of bodies lay bloated with sea water with no one willing to provide them a decent cremation. I saw them again, as also members of both the Communist parties, in the 1984 at the rehabilitation camps for Sikhs following the massacre, providing the inmates with comfort and succour while quietly promoting their ideology.

A bleaker side of the RSS, and the largest show of Hindu chauvinism, was however the anti-cow slaughter campaign in 1966. Then the diehard Hindu group supported by various Shankaracharyas demanded a complete ban on cow slaughter, on the strength of the Directive Principles of State Policy section of the Constitution. When Prime Minister Indira Gandhi rejected their demand, a mob of approximately 10,000, led by the Naga sadhus, clothed only in ash at their splendid naked best, surrounded Parliament House along with hundreds of cows. Prevented from entering Parliament, the mob rampaged through the city and the first 48-hour curfew was ordered. Gulzarilal Nanda, the then home minister, accepted responsibility for the total breakdown of law and order and resigned. We of course were titillated to see in the newspaper photographs of so many naked men and observe that penises came in different shapes and sizes, and learnt too that cows could be effective tools of protest.

- 6 -

High Jinks and a Nurturing Environment

My school had grown organically with us. From four rooms in a house in Kitchener Road to a slightly larger space when the nuns rented an entire house on the same road, we finally found our permanent home with sports and parade grounds to boot. Our growth graphs were so interlinked that quite frequently we were unable to distinguish the difference. We felt we were extensions of one another, except of course occasionally when we locked horns. We stretched the rules, eager to exercise our fledgling wings, fully aware that they could easily be clipped by the authorities. My 'gang' of friends and I believed that rules were made to be broken and it was a measure of our ingenuity not to get caught. We had to our advantage the smug nonchalance of being 'old students'

as most of the nuns who had taught us in junior school were still around.

As we progressed from class to class we were regularly reminded by our delightful and sage principal that the purpose of being in Carmel Convent was not

In the School Play "Wedding at Cana".

The Annual Day Upper Kindergarten Play.

just learning the three Rs – any school could teach us that — but being provided a nurturing environment, being encouraged to think out of the box, assume challenges, and come up tops. I took her advice very literally by working hard for one term every year to rank among the first three students in the class. This was my time-tested strategy to reassure my parents and teachers that I did have it in me to excel in academics. The rest of the school term I would devote myself to my principal objective for going school: to have fun. That this strategy did not altogether work in my favour in class 8 is another matter. Many hours were spent on the playground marching to *Colonel Bogey's*, practising for yet another Republic or Independence Day celebration, engaging in debates, theatre, elocution contests, sports, and even dance classes. The Mangalorean nun who taught us singing had insisted, for some inexplicable reason, which we suspected to be a childhood fantasy, that the school must employ a dance master to teach us Scottish reels and classical waltzes. Notwithstanding this brief, the master unfortunately extended it by trying to teach us the tango. We instinctively knew that this was highly irregular and felt awkward when partnering him. At the same time, it was an exciting moment as we were complicit in this daring act. Unfortunately for him, he was discovered in class 9 by our music nun who had sneaked into the room just when he was bending over a friend of mine, before pulling her back into his arms.

Almost before we knew it, he had been marched out, writing an epitaph to our dance classes.

No one crammed in those days or had tutors or broke down under the stress of exam pressure. The tension of not receiving admission to the right college with the

subject of our choice did not remotely cross our parents' minds, and was certainly not a matter of concern to us. Our supreme confidence was bolstered by the huge class difference between the English-speaking students and those who were from vernacular schools. 'That lot,' we believed, went to engineering colleges or applied to the science streams. Among us, those who wished to become scientists and engineers felt that they faced no competition whatsoever.

My parents, and many like them, were dismayed at this chasm that was developing between the English-speaking and vernacular schools; government and private schools. An almost insurmountable divide was developing between the urban Indian and the rural Indian. My mother's method of salvaging a modicum of egalitarianism was to make it very clear to her children that the household staff was meant to serve her and not us. Apart from education, food and clothing, every other comfort we enjoyed was a privilege and one that could be taken away faster than the blink of an eye.

Ten was our 'coming of age year'. We were expected to iron our school uniforms, make our beds, and polish our own shoes. My brothers' needlework was

The chosen ones after performing a 'respectable dance'—The Scottish Reel (1964).

far superior to mine. During the summer holidays, if we stayed in Delhi we were encouraged to earn our pocket money by washing cars in our neighbourhood. Looking back, I do believe that we, the first generation born post-Independence who were from the 'privileged class' (as they would be defined), were growing up to become obnoxious snobs, positioning ourselves within a charmed circle of exclusivity. It seemed as if we had almost organically inherited all the class prejudices inherent in the system which we had unfortunately bought lock, stock, and barrel from our old masters.

My gang of friends and I had mastered the art of 'not getting caught'. That was so till the day came when I decided to lead a gaggle of girls during school hours to Keventer's ice cream factory situated in close proximity to the school. The plan was to simply walk out of the school gate on the pretext that we were being sent out on an errand. The chowkidar called our bluff and locked the gate. Without a moment's hesitation, we jumped over the gate with the less athletic clambering over it, giving brief, tantalizing glimpses of their totally sexless blue bloomers, an archaic uniform regulation. The manager of the Keventer factory had never experienced anything like this. He kept repeating: 'Such courage and spirit and that too in uniform.' He welcomed us with great style, showed us around, and generously invited us to consume as many ice creams as we wished. Life was simple, innocent, and secure. We had never heard of or been cautioned about molestation, eve-teased, or felt how terrifying it could be to be among a factory full of men. However, the sheer audacity of our act struck us when we tried to sneak back, to be confronted by a battery of dragon ladies with smoke issuing from their nostrils. I am still confused at the gist of the intense 20 minute lecture we received in Mother Superior's room. Whether we were reprimanded for having flouted the rules of good conduct or because some of the girls had inadvertently exposed their bloomers to the eyes of the world, the world comprising one puny chowkidar. The punishment really pinched, as our parents were advised to confiscate all our pocket money for six months so that those in our class who had been 'good' could be treated by us to ice creams. No threat of expulsion, no lasting mark of 'delinquent' behaviour but a sensible creative punishment, which taught us the value of sharing.

We loved going to school, and morning assemblies

were inspiring. The chorus would sing in praise of God and Jesus, and after the morning prayers one of us would read out excerpts of current affairs from a newspaper. If any student had a particularly encouraging piece of news to share she would be invited to do so. All were encouraged to participate.

I was a total misfit in a few classes and would quite frequently be sent down to Mother Superior's office as a punishment. The Hindi and Sanskrit teachers were particularly prone to do so because neither of whom had an iota of humour and imagination. Mother Blanda would look at me and shake her head. When she was not preoccupied with something, our conversation would meander towards my pet obsession. Lucifer, the fallen archangel who was once God's favourite was now my hero. I saw him not as evil but as a bright shining star with superior intellect and beauty. So what if he flouted God's authority? Wasn't this a natural impulse for someone with superior intellect: to question, provoke, find satisfactory explanations, I would ask Mother Blanda this, and to her credit this wonderful Catholic nun did not find my passionate defence of Lucifer blasphemous but instead she rationally advanced counter-arguments.

These exhilarating sessions opened up a plethora of questions, confusion: the notion of Good versus Evil. I was unwilling to accept the obvious explanations and many years later, when reading Ghazali, I remembered that lovely nun who had been so patient with me. Ghazali's arguments coincided with those of Mother Blanda: all that happens is 'His will'.

We also loved being witness to the slightly flirtatious behaviour of the nuns when Father Joseph from St Xavier's visited them. It humanized them in our eyes. This was particularly so after the school took us to see *The Nun's Story* and we all fell in love with the enchanting Audrey Hepburn. Our overriding ambition for the next six months was to become nuns and we went around with folded hands attempting to glide rather than walk, till we realized how ridiculous we looked. The only other expedition to the cinema was, appropriately, to see *The Ten Commandments*.

Our student lives once again became predictable, replete with innocent fun and routine. That was until a curious rumour began floating around the corridors and entered our classrooms, distracting us all, including the teachers. There hung a heavy shroud of secrecy over the school: one of the senior girls was pregnant (she returned to sit for her final exams). We held our second, very grave Assembly (the first was on the day Mother Blanda informed us that the Chinese had attacked our borders). Classes 9, 10, and 11 now had to attend special moral and character building classes conducted by the

same Father Joseph we had seen flirting with the nuns. We were taught about the birds and the bees, bodily changes, attraction to the opposite sex, temptation, and how to resist becoming a 'fast girl'. Most of us were more bewildered than enlightened after the two days of lectures. The only fun was when he encouraged us to ask questions by writing them anonymously on pieces of paper. One of the advantages of having an elder brother was to act as a sounding board for his thoughts on many subjects, including homosexuality. This was indeed very central to his being as he was then reading Jean Genet and grappling with Marcel Proust. Therefore my question in the moral science class was just that: why does the Church regard homosexuality to be a sin? The next day, without alluding to my particular question, we were subjected to a thundering sermon on 'Animals have seasons, Man has reasons,' and the purpose of marriage is procreation. That is 'God's Will' which it is not for us to question.

Procreation was a subject that two of my best friends and I were going to hear more about. Within the next six months we had our second and third sessions on sex education. Over the lunch table a friend's mother decided

Greeting the Bishop of Delhi, Mother Blanda to his left, 1968.

to tackle the complex notions of sex, adult love, desire, and the purpose of menstruation. Lunch took a very long time to digest. A few weeks later we were summoned to have tea with another friend's formidable aunt. She began her 'class' by drawing the penis in three different stages of arousal, which caused us to immediately stop eating and listen to her in awe. Her concluding words of advice to three very impressionable 15 year old virgins was: 'And never say "No" to your husband, whether in the shower or on the chandelier.'

Following that, we discovered D.H. Lawrence and *Lady Chatterley's Lover*, banned worldwide, nestled between Thomas Hardy and Charles Dickens in a friend's father's library. The next four 'day spend' after school was orchestrated to get acquainted with Mr Lawrence. We would wait for her father to return to his army headquarters office, her mother to retire for an afternoon siesta, and then dive into *LCL,* as we called it. Nothing, not even those graphic drawings, had prepared us for this. The only discordant note was struck by the daughter of the house who expressed disgust, not at the description of the ardent love-making but at Lady C 'doing it' with the *mali*.

School life once again settled down to a regular rhythm, only interrupted by the periodic anticipation of an exciting 'treat'. The most exceptional of these was the annual visit to the circus. Our favourite was Gemini, which travelled all the way from Kerala or Madras – much the 'same thing' in our perception, to the extreme annoyance

Class of 1968, Carmel Convent.

of our south Indian friends. The circus pitched its tents with the animal enclosures in the sprawling Parade Ground in Old Delhi. A week prior to the event even the stern Math teacher abandoned all pretence of teaching us, with our attention span down to thirty seconds. The clowns, the ringmaster who brilliantly performed with tigers and lions, the amazing trapeze artists ... we just could not get enough of it all. Most spectacular of them all was however the daring motorcyclist, popularly called Mr Zorro, who would shoot out of a cannon, jump on a motorbike and rev up this throbbing machine to great speed. After circling the entire circumference of the rink, vanished into the wilderness, or so we believed. It was all too magical, till the year the Russians came with their state circus and we, thanks to our communist uncle, were fortunate to get privileged seats. 'Quiet ironical,' a small voice kept tom-tomming in my head. I had to confront my uncle about playing favourites. It was not quite a communist thing to do, I said, to be favouring nephews and niece. He just laughed it off and walked off. Nonetheless, my fledgling sense of justice did not prevent me from being spellbound. No one in the audience had ever seen anything like that. The Russians completely seduced not only our 'Left intellectuals' but all the plebeians, wannabe capitalists, and the fence-sitters throughout that exuberant evening.

Unfortunately, we were unable to savour our excitement and pleasure for long. A week after the grand show another disquieting rumour began filtering into the senior classrooms and the teachers went about their business with grim faces. Our maths teacher had attempted suicide: heated debates sprang up dividing best friends into two warring camps. There were those who believed it to have been a sin and others who viewed it as an act of great courage. I was of the opinion that it was an individual choice to live or die. This business of God's will was hogwash and if argued to its illogical conclusion then suicide was also His will as no act could be performed without His sanction. Was I being prescient? Many years later I would sadly be intimately confronted with the tragic needlessness of suicide.

The dancing policeman was another welcome distraction. He was discovered by an aspiring cub reporter at an obscure intersection directing traffic. Just one photograph in a leading newspaper with a brief write-up catapulted him into the realm of celebrity, albeit fleetingly. He was posted to Vijay Chowk so that the world could admire the graceful execution of his duties as a traffic cop. His exhilaration in the performance of his duties was infectious and evoked spontaneous smiles from all who waited for him to signal Stop or Go. He swung and pirouetted, his arms and hands in complete harmony with the internal rhythm of his body. The sequence of movements was so infectious that we quite frequently begged my father to park near India Gate so that we could execute our own versions of the dancing policeman.

We looked forward to our father's tours as a meeting in Calcutta meant individual boxes of Flury's chocolates for the three of us. I ate mine with great frugality, my elder brother ate all his within 48 hours, and the youngest would willingly share his with us. 'Shows who you are,' my mother would comment. My father's invitations to attend workshops, seminars, and meetings abroad would send us into a frenzy of excitement. Wish-lists were drafted, edited, and finally checked by the dragon lady. Blue denim jeans, a most prized possession, topped the list. Records, Rayban sunglasses, go-go glasses in the late 1960s-early '70s. Can-can half slips were popular because they enabled our skirts to perpetually retain a puffed appearance. Cosmetics, underclothes, chocolates, cheese, sardines, ham ... the list could be stretched to infinity. These lists continued to be compiled till the 1980s but by the mid-1990s they came to an abrupt end. That was when Prime Minister Narasimha Rao launched a series of economic and social reforms with the assistance of his able finance minister, Manmohan Singh, and imported goods began filtering in.

The Chinese betrayal was behind us but dinner table conversations at home were more sombre with the edit pages of newspapers airing critical views of the government, of Krishna Menon, and Nehru's handling of the war. There were enormous food shortages and we seemed to be on the brink of many major disasters. Adult discussions would begin and end with 'after Nehru who?' There were no satisfactory answers. Closer to home, the Akali Dal, spearheaded by Master Tara Singh and the SPGC, were launching another phase of campaigning for a separate *suba* or region within Punjab for the Sikhs.

- 7 -

Tussles for Succession, the Indo-Pak War of 1965, and the Punjab Imbroglio

The summer holidays of 1964 had just began, and we had barely arrived in Shimla when we heard the news that our first prime minister, loved even by those who may not have agreed with him, had died of a massive stroke at 2 p.m. on 27 May. The silence enshrouding us was deafening, akin to the deathly silence just prior to an earthquake. My father was immediately ordered back to Delhi, as were all senior bureaucrats who were then posted in Delhi. My mother decided that there wasn't any reason for us to stay behind so we all returned to a very sombre Delhi. En route, we saw people huddled in groups, crying, weeping. There was little doubt that for that day and the following couple of days the deep pain felt by his daughter, Indira Gandhi, and other immediate relatives found an echo in the hearts of all Indians.

After a seven day special session of Parliament on that fateful day, Gulzari Lal Nanda, the home minister, was sworn in as the caretaker prime minister. The troika of K. Kamaraj (President of the Congress party and generally known as the kingmaker), S. Nijalingappa, and Atulya Ghose were either in a stupor at the shock (to give them the benefit of doubt) or were busy hatching an intriguing, long-term political strategy because they did not think it fit to nominate Gulzari Lal Nanda as the prime minister, and resolved to appoint Indira Gandhi in the belief that she would be a malleable puppet in their hands.

An enormous cloud of fear seemed to have darkened all our lives, as adults huddled together whispering to one another a false sense of reassurance that 'all would be well'. We children clung to each other because this was the closest encounter with death we had experienced. Our beloved Chacha Nehru was dead. We sensed the tension in the air and felt unprotected because, for once, there was no adult supervision from the distance or in our midst.

On the day of the funeral, 28 May, we sat huddled in front of our radio listening to the mellifluous voice of Melville de Mello and the rich baritone of Surijit Sen's commentary on the funeral procession. Their vivid description of the despair on the faces of thousands of Indians who were accompanying the funeral cortege of the prime minister to his final destination had us all weeping silently. He was to be cremated at Shantivana on the banks of the River Jamuna. Although he was affectionately called Panditji, he was certainly no pandit in the Brahminical definition of one. Ironically, even this powerful man, an agnostic who had been at the helm of India for 17 years, was unable to control the manner of his final farewell to his beloved country. Instead, his funeral took a formal traditional Hindu form and ritual, before being consigned to the flames. However, even within the stranglehold of priests we heard a choir singing 'Raghupati Raghav Raja Rama', the bhajan universally indentified with Mahatma Gandhi, and were comforted.

Unlike Gandhi, Nehru departed without appointing a successor. The Pandora's box was cracking at its seams and covert ambitions spilling out. Whispers of unholy alliances were circulating and Indira Gandhi's name as her father's successor, or in this case heir, became the most popular choice. She however showed her true mettle, supported by K. Kamaraj, the president of the Congress party, and chose Lal Bahadur Shastri as the second prime minister of this vast country. For us children, the excitement, discussions, the frayed tempers of my parents and their close friends who seemed, more often than not, to congregate at our home, distracted us from the gloom and despond of the past fortnight. We sat quietly at their feet taking it all in.

The announcement that Lal Bahadur Shastri would be India's next prime minister evoked a collective sigh of relief from most Indians. He was sworn in on 9 June 1964. My younger brother and I were unable to comprehend our parents' enthusiasm and relief, with my mother proclaiming: 'Thank God it is not one of those power-grabbers'. Father sat us down and patiently explained that the stature of a person should not be measured by physical appearance but through his strength of

character, an inclusive sensibility, clear vision, and a deep commitment to take the country forward. As railway minister, Shastri had accepted complete responsibility for a train accident that had occurred in Tamil Nadu although, as Nehru had said in parliament, while accepting his resignation, Shastri was not to be blamed or responsible for the mishap. His resignation was accepted only as an example of constitutional propriety. He took the oath as the prime minister at a very critical juncture in independent India's history. There were huge food shortages due to agricultural shortfalls in many parts of the country and morale was at a low ebb. Pakistan, sensing India's vulnerability and underestimating Shastri's strengths and clear intellect, had initiated large-scale incursions into Kashmir, challenging India to respond, and confident of victory.

1965 began with a call from the new prime minister for people to sacrifice one meal a day to enable the rations to be distributed to the poor as many parts of India were reeling under severe drought. He himself, together with his family set an example in doing so. The response was overwhelming and even restaurants voluntarily downed their shutters on Monday evenings. Restrictions were

Lal Badhur Shastri being sworn in as Prime Minister by President Sarvepalli Radhakrishnan, 1964 (Courtesy: PIB).

placed on the number of dishes that could be served at weddings and other celebratory gatherings and violations fined. He encouraged citizens to convert their lawns into kitchen gardens. We saw photographs of him ploughing the soil to plant crops in his prime-ministerial home. When anti-Hindi agitations in Madras threatened to turn violent, Shastri assured them that English would remain a parallel language of the Government of India. The severity of the crises besetting Shastri's new government was reflected in soaring food prices, shortage of essential medicines, and an overall sense of joylessness for a majority of Indians. Fortunately, our lives continued in its normal tenor, underlain by the usual teenage anxieties and excitements. We wholeheartedly embraced meatless days because it made us feel that we were contributing to the national exchequer.

In the midst of all this gloom and doom, All India Radio sprung a most welcome surprise. Delhi was going to be hooked to television, till now only known of through *Archie* comics and a few Hollywood films. My father was given a JK television set because the company needed to test their product and receive 'reliable' feedback. The programmes were telecast for only two hours from 6 p.m.

to 8 p.m. Most of them were educational documentaries, and a special one for farmers called *Krishi Darshan*, and, of course, the daily news. On Wednesdays they telecast *Chitrahaar,* old Hindi film songs. For the first time we saw a lady newsreader, Pratima Puri, who became an instant star with her charm, elegant diction, and the charming twinkle in her eye when she bade her audience goodnight. The TV set faltered at regular intervals to our great disappointment and the engineer had to be summoned almost every day. We seemed to have almost all the inhabitants of the flats in our crescent sitting glued together like sardines at our home, fascinated by the non-happenings on the screen. The domestic servants had to take turns and my mother actually had an attendance register so that no one missed their turn.

Then came Operation Gibraltar. Frustrated by their failure to gain traction in Kashmir and encouraged by the Chinese 'spanking' of India in 1962, about 30,000 Pakistani army regulars, in civilian garb, came barrelling across the border. The intention was to create general mayhem and incite Kashmiri Muslims to revolt. War was promptly declared. In a macabre sense, it was an exhilarating time. The country was united, patriotism flourished, and we were all on the same side. My brother's friends who had opted for a military career were itching to get their fingers on the trigger. One of them never returned home, and a lane in Defence Colony is named after him. My elder brother, studying at St Stephen's College, joined the Civilian Defence Force, formed to patrol communities and watch out for possible spies and infiltrators. He was disappointed that the volunteers were not issued real weapons but merely long bamboo staves. Every night they would gather on the playground in our community, Satya Marg, and sally forth, patrolling in pairs. They would bang the ground with their staves to scare off potentially well-armed and professionally trained Pakistani infiltrators, and in the process kept everyone up all night. All windows were mandated to be 'blacked out' with dark paper to prevent Pakistani aircraft from identifying bombing targets. The civilian patrol would knock on the doors of violators and issue warnings. All this was like an aphrodisiac: such power in the hands of a college student. Just as in the movies.

The most exciting incident my brother experienced was encountering a sadhu at 2 a.m. one night. While they were talking to him, a Sikh army officer drove up on a Vespa scooter and began interrogating the poor man. He knocked off the sadhu's turban, supposedly to look for hidden weapons, and then ordered him to drop his shorts. The two Stephanians, horrified by the direction of the proceedings, later discovered that as Muslim men are generally circumcised, the officer was employing this unorthodox method of identification. (Needless to say, this somewhat dampened my brother's belief in the Civil Defence Force as an asset on his resume.) He did get a reward, though: a bus trip to the border, a minor ceremony, a handsome certificate, and a surreptitiously scavenged piece of a destroyed Patton tank. Big time hero, my brother. Perhaps the most poignant story that emerged was that of two air force pilots on opposing sides, brothers as it transpired; another sad consequence of an episode that divided families and tore asunder the fabric of communities. Two brothers, one adopted by a relative and transplanted to Pakistan after Partition. As the story goes, the two warring commanders learnt of this and grounded both pilots. After all, the military leaders on both sides had known each other intimately, having studied together at the pre-Independence Imperial Military College, and at the bottom of the imposed overt hostility there remained the seed of a shared history and togetherness.

The war ended, as most modern wars do, in a stalemate. Time, money, and lives lost and no advantage gained by either side. What followed were victory parades in both countries and a never-ending debate on who really won the war. It is said that conquest and domination is naturally built into the human DNA, particularly in the male gender. History was devised to teach humanity how to avoid its own past mistakes. If so, we have failed miserably. No one really believed that this was the 'Last Tango' between these two countries.

However, while the country was at war, I was into my first real 'crush'. He would join the band of night vigilantes and often sleep in my brother's room as it was too early to go home and wake up his family. He was the sleeping beauty and I the prince. The sad thing was that the furthest I got was an exchange of surreptitious glances.

The Tashkent accord was signed on 10 January 1966. We were all glued to the radio and heard that the agreement had been signed after some hard negotiations under the aegis of the Russian prime minister Alexei

Shastri greeting welcoming crowds in Tashkent, 1966 (Courtesy: PIB).

Kosygin. According to it, India agreed to return all Pakistani territory won by brave soldiers at great cost of life and Pakistan pledged never to use overt or covert force against India. They agreed that there would be no future recourse to war, and all disputes would be settled on the basis of peaceful negotiations and mutual benefit. 7,000 people had died during the 22 days of war.

For me, it was anger and disappointment: a young girl who could not see beyond the death of hundreds of soldiers. I spontaneously said: 'Such a senseless war;

General Ayub Khan and Lal Bahadhur Shastri at Tashkent, 1966 (PIB).

I hope when I wake up in the morning I see headlines in the newspaper announcing that both Lal Bahadur Shastri and General Ayub Khan are dead.' The following morning, 11 January 1966, my brother angrily shook me awake and called me a witch, thrusting the newspaper at me. Our valiant prime minister, who had inspired the nation to rally around his slogan 'Jai Jawan, Jai Kisan' had died sometime during the night of a massive heart attack. The conspiracy theories surrounding his death bore the same unresolved arguments as those spun around the mysterious disappearance of Subhas Chandra Bose.

Indira Gandhi was now the natural choice for all the Congress power brokers. As we were informed by my mother, to choose any of the other national leaders would have certainly meant a split in the Congress party. Who knew then, certainly not the troika, that, that was precisely what would happen two years into Indira Gandhi's tenure as prime minster? In just two years from her first tremulous address to the nation she seemed to have grown into her father's shoes but it was never a snug fit and she was perhaps herself conscious throughout her 19 years in the public eye that he would

Prime Minister Indira Gandhi.

have disapproved of her autocratic style of functioning.

Our dinner debates began being coloured by open rebellion on the part of my elder brother who had just joined college and felt he should no longer be subject to parental guidance. His monopoly of the telephone, which was primarily intended for my parents' use, and only secondarily for the children, created huge tensions between him and our mother. There was no question of acquiring a second telephone as connections were at a premium. For non-government personnel that wait could be any period ranging between one and ten years. The game of who knew whom to curry favour with was constantly being played out. From telephone lines and directories, to ration cards, gas connections, and cement and steel permits for house construction, to buying a new car ... everything was scarce. The choice of cars was between Ambassador, Fiat, and Standard Herald, the last–named the preference of the more dashing as it could be turned into a convertible. Despite the grumbling, irritation, and at times loud protests, we accepted the scarcity of commodities as one of the negative fallouts of a young independent nation, labelled a Third World country among many other appelations.

Indira Gandhi's two stints as prime minister generated so much heat around our table that we now had to abide by debating rules rather than free-flowing conversation. The first major setback to India under her stewardship was to succumb to World Bank pressure to devalue the rupee. I am certain it was this one singular capitulation to the World Bank that germinated the seeds of mistrust and lifelong suspicion of and hostility towards the World Bank and the Ford Foundation. Her natural inclination to be suspicious and paranoid about those she perceived to be hostile to her personally and to India at large did not assist her efforts to build strong bridges with the US, which subsequently let her and India down at every vulnerable juncture. In February 1967, after the fourth general election, she was obliged to accept Morarji Desai as deputy prime minister, in what was 'not the most compatible marriage' as my mother put it. We bowed to her judgement as she herself was soon becoming the queen of incompatibility, especially in terms of her marriage. Her passionate support of Indira Gandhi, 'the no-nonsense lady', was reaching such levels that Indira Gandhi was becoming her alter ego. The only flea in the ointment was that Indira Gandhi had the world, and more specifically India, as her stage, while mother had to content herself with her limited constituency: her house, us, and the source of all her troubles, my father and his mother.

Indira Gandhi stamped a distinct 'Indira imprint' by breaking from the established order and functioning of governance. She introduced a 10-point programme, which encompassed the nationalization of Indian banks, coal, steel, copper mining, refineries, cotton textiles, and insurance. She split the Congress party not once but twice. She granted statehood to Meghalaya, Manipur, and Tripura; NEFA was declared a Union Territory and renamed Arunachal Pradesh. No one, barring the upholders of universal human rights and territorial integrity questioned the annexation of Sikkim. She abolished the privy purses and privileges of the maharajas. The Land Ceiling Act, a compulsory version of Vinobha Bhave's Bhoodan movement, was adopted, housing for landless labour and abolition of bonded labour formed part of her ambitious programme.

In 1966, with political pressure rising to a climax following the Indo-Pakistan War of 1965, where thousands of Sikh officers and soldiers in the Indian army had displayed enormous valour in defending the country, Prime Minister Indira Gandhi, Nehru's daughter, acceded to the demand for a separate state of Punjab. This was created on 1 November.

•

Going back in time, throughout the 1950s and '60s the leader of the Sikhs, Master Tara Singh, had struggled to resurrect the promised 'homeland'. In 1960 the Sikh masses committed themselves to supporting the Akali Dal and Masterji, and with their support he launched his last decisive *morcha* to pressurize the central government to fulfil their pre-Independence pledge. Masterji was arrested in May 1960 and jailed in Dharamshala. The *morcha* intensified after his arrest and the properties of many important Sikh personalities committed to the cause were seized, and the businesses of many came to a standstill. The productivity of Punjab was at its lowest ebb. That notwithstanding, the government stood firm, deliberately making provocative speeches against the Sikhs which led Sant Fateh Singh, deputy *jathedar* of the Alkali Dal, to undertake a fast unto death. At the advice of Pratap Singh Kairon, Master Tara Singh was released and warned that he would be held responsible for the Sant's death. This deliberate provocation spurred Masterji to declare that if the Sant died he would himself undertake a fast unto death. The tense situation in Punjab eventually motivated Nehru to make a statement to the press that linguistic principles would be applied to Punjab in all sincerity and the Sikhs would not be discriminated against on any account. With this assurance the Sant broke his fast.

The Sant and a section of the Akali Dal may have been satisfied by Nehru's statement of intent to the press. That however was not the case with the Sikh people, who had voluntarily subjected themselves to immense hardship during the *morcha* during which 57,000 of them had been jailed and felt utterly let down by their leaders. The credibility of the Akali Dal had sunk its lowest ebb. It was at that crucial juncture that Masterji, on 15 August 1961, went on a hunger strike, pledging an oath at the Akal Takht to fast unto death for a Punjabi *suba*. His advisors, fearing communal clashes between the Sikhs and Hindus of Punjab, persuaded him to break his fast on the 44th day on the basis of mere verbal assurances from the prime minister. I awoke that day to see a picture on the front page of the *Statesman* of my great uncle drinking *nimbu-pani* mixed with honey from a glass held by Sant Fateh Singh. The fast was over and with that began the decline in Masterji's influence and his moral authority.

He had to face the wrath of the Sikh community for breaking his oath to the Akal Takht, and to atone for this sin the Gurudwara Prabhandak Committee decreed that he was to clean the shoes of devotees visiting the Golden Temple. No big deal as a regular practice of *seva*, but as a punishment it was. We, as a family, were heartbroken to see a man of great integrity, selfless devotion to his country and community, cleaning shoes in the Golden Temple, to atone for his 'sin'. A man who, notwithstanding his access to great power, never exploited it for personal gain. During his lifetime his family had not added an iota to their property or wealth unlike many Punjab leaders who had used their positions for personal aggrandizement. Pratap Singh Kairon may have been a strong, capable administrator of Punjab but his reputation as one of the most corrupt Congress leaders eventually led to one of his most ardent supporters, Jawaharlal Nehru, turn away from him.

Venality is a characteristic of the Akali leaders of today, who appear to be more committed to retention of power than a commitment to the Panth. A deep chasm was created between the Sikhs and the Hindus in Punjab and tensions between the two communities was palpable. The Nehru-Kairon nexus had won the battle, the Akali Party split into two, and this undoubtedly diminished Master Tara Singh's political stature.

Imprisoned again in 1966 under the Defence of India Act for his statement: 'Punjabi *suba* of my dream is a homeland for the Sikhs which would be accorded special status under Article 370.' For this he was considered unpatriotic and anti-national. This was his last stint in jail. He died on 22 November 1967. Two years later, in 1969, Darshan Singh Pheruman went on a hunger strike demanding the incorporation of all the remaining Punjabi-speaking areas, particularly Chandigarh, in the new state of Punjab. He died on the 74th day of his fast. Indira Gandhi accepted the Akali demand for an independent state on linguistic lines. The existing state was trifurcated into the Sikh-majority Punjab, which included the Sikh holy city of Amritsar. The southern Hindu-majority areas were divided into the states of

Himachal Pradesh and Haryana. Many Akali Dal leaders believe it had been a mistake to divide Haryana because the majority of the northern districts had a large Sikh population. Is the chapter on the Sikhs closed? For the moment, yes, and I pray it remains so, for I hear the drumbeat of communalism sounding again and despair that secularism has been deeply wounded, perhaps mortally, in India.

The Pahari-speaking hilly areas of Punjab formed Himachal Pradesh. Chandigarh was declared a Union Territory to be shared as the capital of both Punjab and Haryana. My grandfather termed it the final death-knell of Punjab, first split into two, and now into three states. The divisions and declaration of Chandigarh as a Union Territory was in the nature of a colonial master-stroke, aimed at keeping the fault lines simmering.

•

For us, as members of the 'trendy set', dinner at a dhaba in the new Haryana was the 'in' thing to do. In 1973 came the nationalization of oil after Caltex and Burmah Shell refused to supply petrol to the armed

Statue of Master Tara Singh near Parliament House, New Delhi (Courtesy: Tejbir Singh).

forces in the war of liberation of East Pakistan. This last act contributed to Indira Gandhi's Durga image, post the liberation of East Pakistan and its rebirth as Bangladesh.

Indira Gandhi's autocratic methods of functioning, with an utter disdain for propriety split our teetering nuclear family into two. My father believed that her autocratic, non-inclusive style of functioning, her preference for the advice of her 'kitchen cabinet' which frequently overrode official counsel, undermined institution-building, and spawned unhealthy personal ambitions within the bureaucracy, with senior officials openly currying favour. My mother accused my father of being a male chauvinist and celebrated what she believed was getting rid of deadwood and the power-grasping old guard of the Congress. Poor Kamaraj was viewed by her as the greatest villain post-1947. I added my two-bit support to father, my elder brother, too engrossed in the joys and heartache of his first serious love affair, had nothing to say, and my younger brother loved Mrs G's resemblance to the Queen of Hearts and swished around an imaginary sword imperiously intoning 'Off with her/his head.'.

- 8 -

College, Gaiety, Naxalism, and the High Life

The winds of change blew equally swiftly in our personal lives as in the political and social spheres. At one instant we were schoolgirls and in the next had been transformed into college students. We sailed through admission interviews and other formalities, never in doubt of getting admission in a college and subject of our choice. Mine was Lady Sri Ram and I chose Philosophy, which seemed to sit well with my pseudo-intellectual pretensions. We, the privileged, were pushed out into the world of DTC buses, autorickshaws, and those horrible sex-starved Delhi men. Each bus journey was traumatic, not knowing when an 'uncle' was going to lurch at you, or rub against you while moving to make space in an already crowded vehicle. I eventually discovered how geometry could serve as a guardian angel when the compass or divider became our weapon of protection. We strategically learnt to parry any thrust or rub with a sharp counter thrust. Survival instincts, naturally combative temperaments, and disgust at this mass of male hideousness morphed us into a brigade of Ninja Turtles. We discovered something called a Lady Sri Ram Special, DTC buses run for the convenience of shrinking violets too delicate to travel in the normal public transport. We discovered that many such maidens, who we popularly called *bhenjis*, were actually roses in full bloom. They were in the 'vernacular' mould, and we were the snobbish English-speaking smarties. Those were the days when a cross-over in parliament was more frequent than in social circles. Their conversations were peppered with references to boyfriends, and very frequently the bus became a stage on which to master the fine art of flirting. They were the main actors, the conductor and the driver mere male props. While we moved around with the mandatory three or four books, one of which had to be Sartre/Beauvoir, accompanied by Baudelaire, Rimbaud, with the third choice ranging from Dostoevsky to Henry James, they (the *bhenjis*) were robustly embracing their new-found freedom. We tended to move in a herd. Group identity was paramount, with occasional individual flights of fancy. Freedom from parental and school scrutiny opened up multiple choices, and temptation lurked around every corner. The Group bunked college, the Group smoked their first joint, the Group went to afternoon parties rather than attending the boring Indian philosophy class. It was not intrinsically dull but comatose in the way this wonderful subject was communicated, straight out of notes prepared a decade earlier. The Group danced together. I remember being completely floored by a young man in one of those 'illicit' afternoon parties. Sipping rum-spiked Coca Cola, he declared, when discussing Samuel Becket, that if he had not 'made a name' in the literary world by the age of 30 he would kill himself. He still lives as an upper middle-class bourgeois sipping his single malt and pontificating on the state of the nation.

Drugs and marijuana, sexual freedom, Bohemian life-styles, a rediscovery of Hindu spiritualism, in particular and Orientalism in general ... all these came together around the same time to define 'the generation of "68'. Youth from across the world meeting in the most unlikely places would be connected by their dress-style, their outlook, the music to which they related, the books they had or were reading. If you were not at Woodstock yourself but your music included The Doors, Jimi Hendrix, Creedence Clearwater Revival, Janis Joplin, Bob Dylan, and Don McLean, you were one of us. As you were too if you recognized the term 'Street-Fighting Years', 'Soul on Ice', *The Wretched of the Earth*. Also, if you were aware that it was Tariq Ali and the 22 March Movement; or it was Elridge Cleaver and the Black Panthers with their militant Black Power movement.

Meeting friends at the University Cafe was an exciting date in the diary of a girl from LSR. 'Nothing's happening in our college,' was a common complaint among my friends. I will always remember the day when a friend from Miranda House singled out a good looking young man and whispered 'He's a Naxalite'. Naxalites defined for us romantic heroes who were fighting for the oppressed of rural India. Going underground, dodging police bullets, dropping out of college, living with the 'real people' of India in the villages was revolutionary. We greatly envied those among us who were sufficiently courageous and motivated to opt out of the comfort zone of bourgeois urban backgrounds and dedicate their lives to fighting the injustice perpetuated by the state. Also, the Naxalites I saw in Delhi University were good looking, sexually attractive young men which certainly elevated them sufficiently in our eyes for them to become our heroes.

•

In Bengal, a year earlier, on 24 May, poor landless peasants, agitating for justice, were fired upon by police in a very nondescript *thana* called Naxalbari. That name entered our lexicon forever. This defining incident brought into focus a party, an ideology, and its leadership. A day later, in another incident nearby, police fired on a similar crowd of protestors killing 10, mostly women and children. It was a re-enactment of Chairman Mao's oft-repeated remark: 'A spark had been lit that will light the prairie fire.' This growing cause came to be known as Naxalism after the small Naxalbari police *thana* where it all began, its adherents basing their ideology on Mao's thinking.

Lured by an intellectual commitment to fight oppression, to adventure, and to romanticism, the urban élite joined the Naxalite movement in large numbers and Presidency College in Calcutta became a hotbed for radicalism. Ideology soon developed into violence and Calcutta began to experience a form of guerrilla insurgency. Landlords, police officers, and politicians were favoured targets. Knives were the weapons of choice and terror reigned. Why were innocent traffic policemen standing on a circular platform at the centre of an intersection directing traffic being targetted? It was the question that eventually awakened us to the reality that the Naxalites did not really believe in justice.

In the villages, land was being forcibly occupied by the labourers in a movement openly promoted by the CPM(L). They continued a series of low grade insurgencies as the movement spread to other states and to this day, periodic episodes of violence flare up with a generally disproportionate response by the authorities. Several factions who abandoned armed resistance to join the political mainstream were described as 'sellouts' by the radical fringe. Could this so-called 'revolution' have been successful? Of course not. Did it have the potential to continually fester like a deeply embedded virus that periodically flares up and causes varying levels of discomfort? Absolutely, and it continues to do so.

My elder brother, who had joined Citibank in Calcutta during this time and was witness to *gherao*s had no grand romantic notion of the Naxalite movement. This, in Bengal, was a far reality than just a clutch of students debating, planning, and strategizing total revolution, often high on rhetoric and marijuana. Although the original movement was brutally crushed by the West Bengal government under Chief Minister Siddhartha Shankar Ray, four decades later it has vastly expanded its 'liberated zones'. By official reckoning, these are spread over vast swathes of north-eastern, central, and southern India, covering over 200 districts.

•

I have always wondered how different life in those years would have been had I attended college in the old Delhi University campus. A longer bus ride but certainly a richer and more diverse experience. Connaught Place was conveniently located between the University and

Vinay Marg, and served as an active halfway house for a 'coffee klatch', with friends of both sexes of course. Some of them would hop on to the University Special while we from LSR would travel the more inconvenient route. Occasionally frustrated by the long bus delays, we would hitch a ride. Milk Bar, Bankura, Madras Coffee House, La Boheme, Laguna, Mikado were the most frequent interim destinations.

As much as these years were redolent with discovery, fun, friendships, et al., music was the catalyst that wove this life together. Woodstock happened in 1969, about 12,000 miles from New Delhi, but it had a profound impact on the local scene. Let us first explore the facts. 500,000 people showed up at a meadow in upstate New York to participate in a music festival. It was unadulterated chaos for three days. Who was on stage? Ravi Shankar (yes, the sitar maestro was there and played in the rain), Joan Baez, Jefferson Airplane, Santana, Grateful Dead, The Who, Blood Sweat & Tears, and innumerable others, but none matching the guitar shredding anthem by Jimi Hendrix. Interestingly, Swami Satchidananda kicked off the festival with an invocation. The music filtered across the globe and wafted over India. The bands that missed at Woodstock were prominent too. New names cropped up such as The Doors, Three Dog Night, and many others. My younger brother formed a band called Pebbles and even performed on All-India Radio with covers from The Doors. His theme song was 'Break on Through to the Other Side', little realizing that it would become his personal anthem.

Delhi became an unwilling host for the Hippies or Flower Children en route to Nepal. They were far more welcome in Goa and Madras, and Bombay looked on indulgently. They were the young rebels, mostly from America, who had defied their country's invasion of Vietnam, called themselves pacifists, and were labelled flower children for their belief that the language of flowers was far more effective in engendering peace and happiness than the barrel of a gun. Flowers symbolized beauty, integrity, and happiness, which they sought to spread to the rest of violent humanity. This, preferably accompanied by marijuana with which the younger generation had been experimenting but were now cautiously moving away from, and on to LSD and other amphetamines. The most popular among these were methedrine and mandrax. The hippies had utopian notions of India's all-inclusive spirituality and it was tragic to see many of them being exploited by local pushers, pimps, and cheap hoteliers in Paharganj. For many, visiting a gurudwara for the *langar* was the closest they got to Indian spiritualism.

Disco-dancing was in vogue. My brother returned home one day and after dinner staged a demonstration of the Twist for the family. There was a new student in his class who had just returned from Washington, where her father had been posted with the Indian Embassy, and she had brought home the Twist. We sat transfixed in silence while he twisted and contorted his body and gyrated back and forth, down to the floor and then up again. My mother promptly labelled it 'that vulgar dance' and wanted no further demonstrations in her sanctuary. She advised us to stick to the Fox Trot, and Cha-cha-cha. No wiggling posteriors for her. Discotheques began to sprout in Delhi. The first, The Cellar in Regal Building, transformed our lives. The entire hip and trendy set of Delhi converged outside the narrow door leading down to the basement: literally a cellar. The air was buzzing with excitement as we entered this aesthetically appointed discotheque. Each of us was handed a candle,

Vignettes from The Cellar (Courtesy: Ram Rahman).

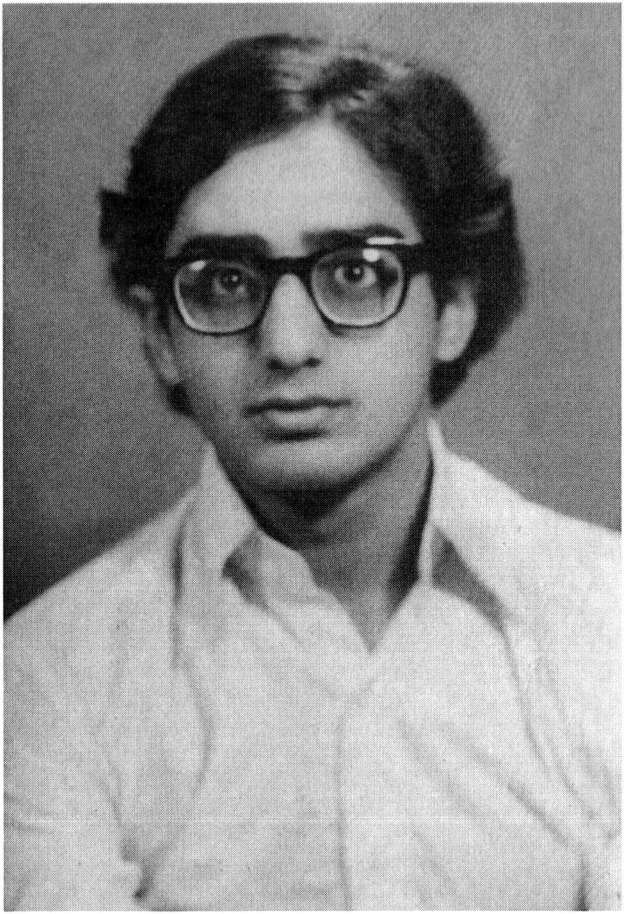

Moni Singh, Delhi, 1971.

encouraged to jump up on the tables and 'smoke-write' our names, or whatever else inspired our creativity, on the ceiling. From that moment we all felt we owned the place: it certainly owned all of us. It never disappointed us in fun-filled evenings of dancing, flirting, with the braver among us surreptitiously lighting up a joint. My group would periodically bunk afternoon classes and hang out in Asylum in Greater Kailash. Another option was Tabela in Intercontinental Hotel (now the Oberoi) for the discerning, upmarket crowd. Parties moved from secret locations to homes under adult supervision with the occasional smuggled liquor. The days of sanitized youth were fast being submerged by the insidious creep of Western mores. A form of cultural globalization, I expect.

Drugs formed part of the culture and tragic endings became the norm, together with suicides and the occasional homicide. An army officer, jilted by his Miranda House girlfriend, shot her fatally at the university coffee shop with his service revolver. My younger brother began a deep downward spiral into drugs which would culminate in his own suicide many years later.

- 9 -

Foreign Shores: Baghdad

A stroke of luck was my father accepting, or more precisely, his Ministry agreeing, to release him for three years in 1969 for a UN assignment in Baghdad. An electric current of excitement shot through our secure family space. My mother, who had read just about every available book on the Mesopotamian civilization, could not believe she would finally see what was left of the Hanging Gardens of Babylon. My younger brother was finally leaving Sri Ram College of Commerce to study in Beirut University. As for myself, I would stay on in Delhi with a dear friend, Ruby Grewal, and her easygoing parents. My elder brother was calculating which of the carpets and furniture he could transport to his first independent flat in Calcutta.

My first summer holiday in Baghdad introduced me

to the realities of a dictatorial state, where democratic principles of governance, which we in India have always assumed to be our birthright, were not even discussed aloud. A city where even a mildly anti-Saddam Hussein conversation had perforce to be conducted in large playgrounds and other open spaces where the state's 'ears' could not overhear what was considered to be seditious. Where the dreaded black car and subsequent knock on the door, usually late at night, was justified as the 'traitor' being invited to the state guest-house. Families were left to die a thousand silent deaths in the hope of seeing a loved one again some day. No official enquiries were encouraged and all information was usually gathered from 'back channels'.

My excitement at meeting my parents and younger brother in Baghdad for the summer vacation after nearly six months of separation was clouded by the several police check-points where AK 47 armed policemen would be nonchalantly pointing their guns at passing cars. These had to slow down to a crawl before being waved on. Never in my wildest imagination could I have foreseen then that one day this would be a common sight in my own country. My Iraqi friends later informed me that

الاسم الانسة برابين كور سينغ

Name Miss. Prabeen Kaur
INGH

الوظيفة كريمة خبير

Title Daughter of an E pert

العنوان مكتب الممثل المقيم لبرنامج التنمية للامم المتحدة

Address Office of the Res
Reprrsentative of
United Nations Develop
Programme, Baghdad

توقيع حامل البطاقة

ignature of the Bearer of the card

وزير الخارجية

Minister of Foreign Affairs

What remains of my Iraqi Identity, Baghdad. The corner was chewed by my dog.

every now and again they would stop a random car ‘for fun’ to allay their boredom. The journey from the airport to our house in Mansour Street (from where Saddam Hussein was eventually flushed out of a tunnel) has left an indelible memory of two men hanging from two poles in the middle of Tahrir Square. The real 'hangman' from our childhood games, was the first thought that crossed my mind before the shock of what I was seeing numbed me into despair. They were suspected spies who were forerunners of an attempted coup, or so we were informed. The practice of displaying bodies of traitors in the most famous public square was common among the dictators of West Asia as a deterrent to other rebels. What shook us all even more was that vehicular traffic, and also pedestrians, went about their businesses as they would on any other day.

Our landlord's wife was the daughter of the last governor of Mosul during the erstwhile ruler's reign. She lived in a house adjacent to its twin lookalike. It was common practice among the affluent to build houses similar to one another so that each wife could have her own identical residence. We, however, never met any Iraqi who had more than one wife. Our landlord's wife would talk to us about their lives during the monarchy, which seemed to us to have been more glamorous and easier, with unrestricted holidays abroad for the affluent. However, life then did not appear to have been any more democratic than under the Ba'athist state of Saddam

New Year Eve celebration in Mansouriya Club, 1970.

Hussein. Most Iraqis did admit grudgingly that the so-called Socialist regime had improved the quality of life for a majority of Iraqis. Their one major constraint was self-censorship. So long as they were not viewed as a threat to the government, the people of Iraq were relatively free to pursue their ambitions. Although a place where by and large privileges were graciously dispensed by the ‘benevolent’ leader, the people generally had it all. This included medical services, education, freedom from any Islamic dogma, especially for women. Art, literature, studio pottery flourished to the degree they could under the aegis of a repressive regime. The young Iraqi students whom we befriended were no different from us. Although their English was not fluent, our common love for Bob Dylan, Joan Baez, Simon & Garfunkel, The Doors, Led Zeppelin connected us, allowing us to develop a language of communication. My brother got in touch with a drug pusher on the second day while walking down to Al Mansouriya Club. I wish I had reported him then to my parents and perhaps put a break on his spiralling descent in later years.

My mother had two ground rules in relation to any overseas postings if her husband wished her to accompany him. Rule one: never stay in an expat colony; she wanted to meet the ‘real people’. Rule two: hire a local cook. Mansour was a colony where affluent Iraqis lived and the Club was a haven for them and us. Tennis, squash, swimming, cards, billiards; all the trappings of the colonial lifestyle were zealously guarded, including a distinct Anglo-Arabic cuisine.

I still recall with clarity the day my father and Saddam Hussein casually greeted each other over whisky bottles. The club allowed its members to deposit their own bottle of alcohol, which incidentally was never adulterated. We were sitting with our Iraqi friends when Saddam Hussein walked in with his cronies, including Tariq Hussein. There was a buzz of excitement and also, an undercurrent of trepidation. He saw my father removing a bottle of Royal Salute from its velvet pouch and sent one of his cronies to enquire what it was. In a spontaneous gesture, my father gave it to him as a gift for the president, who accepted it with a gracious nod and sent back a bottle of Something Special. That evening no one wanted to stay a moment longer than social protocol demanded.

The Hanging Gardens of Babylon were alas a huge disappointment, with a poor crumbling lion keeping vigil over what had once been one of the wonders of the world. The Ctesiphon Arch however impressed us as one of the great engineering feats of history. It was a Mecca for all structural engineers, who would come and bow their heads to honour the genius of past masters. We were introduced to the delights of rowing on the Tigris. The boatman would en route grill delicious *Masgouf*, the national fish of Baghdad, accompanied with warm buttery *Samoon,* an Iraqi bread similar to the baguette. One weekend a month would be spent on our landlord's farms in Mosul gorging on delicious *dolmas*, *kibbies*, goat cheese, olives, and other delicacies. We felt that the Iraqis must be among the most hospitable and generous people in the world. We also learnt quite early never to express appreciation of any trinkets or other precious objects as they would immediately insist we keep whatever it was. They were a proud race, who held their heads high among the Arabs, tracing their roots to the great Mesopotamian civilization, and not the Johnny come lately Gulf Arabs. Indeed, they were very inclusive of the Arab, Jewish, and Christian communities.

My mother was in bliss land, disappearing for hours in the museum, artists' studios, making friends with women from the nascent women's movement. The first UN sponsored conference of women was held in Baghdad. She discovered her fondness for Abraham and even sacrificed a lamb which she had nurtured from its infancy in Sammara. Thanks to her, we saw the mosques at Karbala and Najaf. She tracked down, through her Iraqi connections, the room in which Guru Nanak had stayed during his journey to Mecca. This proved to be a small room in the older part of Baghdad, wedged between the locked rooms of two ancient Sufis. We discovered that the Marsh Arabs referred to Guru Nanak as one of their *pirs*. These were the poor gentle Marsh Arabs who, many years later, were brutally attacked by Saddam Hussein with deadly poison gas and virtually decimated. My mother sought an appointment with the president who, in an amused, benevolent frame of mind, gave her permission to clean the room where Guru Nanak had stayed and offer *ardas* and *prasad* before it was re-locked. It was subsequently to be reopened for the Indian prime minister I.K. Gujral long after we had bade farewell to Baghdad and our friends there. One whom I still remember, Samar, was a beautiful girl who had everyone hopping to her whims but was dearly loved and great fun. She was engaged to her gentle poetic cousin who dreamt of a utopian state where he and Samar would live 'happily ever after'. She however confessed to me that she could never marry him as he was not man enough ... translated to mean 'he could never beat me'. It was a sign of inspired masochism, much admired by many Iraqi women.

- 10 -

Echoes of War

For the people of India, 1971 dawned on a positive note with Indira Gandhi winning a two-thirds majority in the Lok Sabha elections. The Indo-USSR treaty of Peace, Friendship, and Cooperation was signed, much to the delight of both the communist parties. We hung around in coffee houses and discotheques listening to protest songs against the war in Vietnam. A subject of debate was the huge influx of refugees from East Pakistan, after West Pakistan's military crackdown on its own people. This had happened merely because they had lost the general elections to the Awami League of East Pakistan. Tension between India and Pakistan was riding on a very taut string and the Tashkent accord was like the King Crimson song *Epitaph*, 'The wall on which the prophets wrote / Is cracking at the seams / '.

With startling solidarity rarely witnessed in politics, the East Pakistan Awami League had in the national elections more or less won virtually every seat in their wing of Pakistan in the national elections. With an absolute majority in the Pakistani parliament, the winner arrived in Rawalpindi to claim the right to form the government. President Yahya Khan and Prime Minister Zulfikar Ali Bhutto refused to yield power. A crackdown in East Pakistan, led by the military, followed. The Awami League was banned, its leader, Sheikh Mujibur Rahman arrested and transported to West Pakistan. Pogroms were conducted against the civilian population and millions fled across borders to neighbouring Indian states. An armed rebellion struggled to hold its ground having declared independence for East Pakistan.

If this sounds messy and fraught with danger, Pakistan incomprehensibly raised the stakes by launching a pre-emptive strike on Indian air force bases. Shades of the 1967 Middle East war with a hopelessly different outcome. I remember that the Taj Mahal had been camouflaged with burlap draped over a forest of twigs and leaves, the marble glowing no longer as a beacon of light. What then did the Pakistanis name this latest insanity? Operation Chengiz Khan. If they had read the history of the Mongols, they would have known that they, during their 100-year rule, had caused an 11 per cent decline in the world's population. Gentle benefactors of humanity they certainly were not. It was indeed a far cry from the *pak* the Pakistanis adopted as their name. This time, our iron lady, Indira Gandhi, had had enough. The Indian population had understood, if not accepted, the complexities of Kashmir. East Pakistan was a different kettle of fish. Nothing short of total capitulation in the east would be acceptable and Indian forces poured across the western front to exert pressure on Pakistan. Thirteen days after it began, the third Indo-Pakistan war was over. It was an incredible sight to see a Pakistani general surrendering his ceremonial sword to his Indian counterpart in a Dhaka sports stadium. As college kids, we speculated on what the other side must be feeling about the pictures that circulated in the global media. Most of us felt that the two countries had just hit the 'pause' button again, and yes, Kargil did follow many years later.

Geopolitics in the 1970s was heavily influenced by the 'Cold War' protagonists, the Soviet Union and the US.

Lt Gen A.A.K. Niazi signing the Instrument of Surrender under the stern gaze of Lt Gen J.S. Aurora. Standing immediately behind (L-R) Vice Admiral Krishnan, Air Marshal Dewan, Lt Gen Sagat Singh, Maj Gen J.F.R. Jacob (with Flt Lt Krishnamurthy peering over his shoulder. Veteran newscaster, Surojit Sen of All India Radio, is seen holding a microphone on the right, 1971 (Courtesy: PIB).

Nehru's 'Non Aligned Bloc' movement, the intended third power, was formed with trumpets sounding and Roman processional music but, in all honesty, a power bloc which included India, Yugoslavia, Egypt, Ghana, etc.? Really? In any event, the Americans sided with their favourite global allies, military dictators, while the Soviet Union stood by any nation that opposed the Americans. The Chinese, busy with the impending 'rapprochement' with Nixon-led America, largely remained silent observers.

Even then, Nixon urged the Chinese to get involved on the eastern front in some capacity but sensibly the Chinese declined. It was all too late to put Humpty and Dumpty back together again and Pakistan became two countries with the birth of Bangladesh. This was an explicit, undeniable victory and a really proud moment for India. More parades, more speeches, not much time and emotion devoted to the extensive loss of life. That is the macabre nature of war: residual grief for a while followed by another round. It is a truly sad reality that we just cannot seem to learn our lessons, even through our own experiences.

My personal experience of the 1971 war began in Baghdad, where the news of what was happening was shattering for all of us, and for the first time my mother reached out to the ladies in the Indian embassy. Our most accurate source of news was Grp-Capt. Nirmal Suri, head of the squadron of MIG pilots stationed in Baghdad to train Iraqi pilots. The Indian squadron was on high alert, expecting to be recalled to India at a minute's notice. In the midst of what we thought was spontaneous solidarity among all Indians in Baghdad we were shocked at the bigotry displayed by almost all our fellow countrymen towards a Muslim Indian colleague of my father who was on deputation with the UN as an expert in town and country planning. Short of openly accusing him of being a Pakistani spy, these so-called tolerant Indians ostracized him and he soon found all doors shut to him except ours. He came over for lunch every day and we saw this warm, intelligent, highly articulate gentleman slowly retreat into his shell. That is, until my mother broke through his self-imposed mental isolation, and he recovered his sense of black humour.

This attitude was all the more incomprehensible to me as I recalled that in 1966 my elder brother and a close friend had just graduated from St Stephen's College. Infused with boundless youthful fervour, they chose adventure to mint their 'adulthood', deciding to hitchhike all the way to London through the Middle East and Europe. The first stage was however a cargo ship from Bombay to Basra, 'deck class', or as my brother put it, 'the stars above and the deck below'. The M.S. *Sirdhana* made one stop, Karachi. It was like entering forbidden territory the year following the 1965 war. They did not know what to expect from the large number of Pakistani men who boarded the ship on their way to Mecca for Haj.

The shock was that the Pakistanis spoke fluent Punjabi and were friendly and inquisitive. They ragged the Indians about hockey and cricket in a spirit of friendly rivalry, sang Baisakhi bhangra songs, and shared their food. They were also very disappointed to learn that my brother and his friend had never met Raj Kapoor.

Why then the three wars (including 1948) and the constant war-mongering? That toxic mix of religion and politics, the ambitions of men, the lust for conquest and domination, the pursuit of retribution for real and imagined affronts? What drives the collective hate but also the individual acceptance and even admiration? Will it ever end? I survey the global landscape today and see conflict, war, and conflagration everywhere with no visible cause for optimism. The hard intractable attitudes, rejection of functional compromises, dispassionate acceptance of tragedy, wanton destruction, and the complete absence of mercy for children. Is this the moment that divine intervention will resuscitate humanity or has that 'power' too surrendered all hope?

Even so, the 1960s and '70s, with all their dysfunctionality and conflicts, were also decades of exploration and burgeoning maturity as we moved from a secure college existence to the professional world and the pursuit of economic independence. Safe sanctuaries had to be left behind and we had to sustain ourselves. No silver spoons here except for those who naturally gravitated to family businesses.

- 11 -

Marriage, Motherhood, Parenting

I returned to Delhi after spending a year with my parents in Baghdad, excited to be living with my elder brother and his wife. I was embarking on a career in advertising and ready to embrace the real world, I was moving towards becoming financially independent when an unexpected unease overtook me. 'Twenty-one and never been kissed'. This alas was the constant refrain of my worldly-wise sister-in-law, a natural coquette. 'Whom are you waiting for? A knight on a white charger to rescue the princess in the ivory tower?' inquired my dearest friends in exasperation.

The truth was that I had a script in my head and was looking for the 'right hero' to play the part. All the young men we partied with did not really fit the role. Yes, there were the odd flirtations, the sudden tell-tale blush but I was not going to succumb to anyone except my hero. Where was he? Definitely looking for me. I was the epitome and product of the far-reaching influence of Mills and Boon, the popular romance books of my generation. I did not get to read many of them but the pivotal role they played in shaping my idea of the ideal romance was far greater than anything espoused in *Wuthering Heights* or Mary McCarthy's *The Group*. Most of my group friends were either married or in 'steady relationships', with marriage most certainly the end agenda. Wherever I looked, marriage, love, passion, were the subjects of endless discussion, as were requited/unrequited love, yearning, tears, sudden spurts of joy and happiness. From heady college life where we fiercely held on to our individuality, all around me I now saw the same friends who felt they were not complete without the 'other'. Life for them was defined by what 'he' or 'she' said. Was I the freak or had a great deal changed during the year I was away? The most intense political discussions or serious debates on art and literature would invariably turn to the 'man-woman relationship'. Oh my god, I thought, give me a break.

That was until the day an acquaintance from the

past caught up with me on his scooter at a traffic light. I vaguely remembered him as someone I could always laugh with: amusing, a touch foppish; the type you did not take seriously. Telephone numbers were exchanged and I promptly forgot about him. The next day he called and continued to do so till I agreed to see a film with him. A more devoted 'suitor' did not exist. He succeeded in the next couple of months to present himself at all the social evenings I attended. He waited endlessly outside my office to drop me home, much to the delight of my boss who took great pleasure in making me work late. All the while my boss would casually gaze out of the window and comment 'He is still waiting'. He soon began to crowd my life much to the delight of my friends, although they felt that endless conversations on current political scenarios and the inequitable distribution of resources and arguments on what constitutes fine art and kitsch were not exactly 'lover like' or conducive to moving in that direction. That continued till one day B brought over his much-thumbed *Collected Poems of W.H. Auden.*

We began to do silly flirty things, running around Nehru Park in the rain, singing old film songs to each other, exchanging nonsensical little notes. Soon we began to be counted as a couple. He was not however the hero of my script. Could this really be love? I guess it did seem like it. Peer pressure decreed that I should have a dinner party so that they could collectively evaluate the situation and pass a verdict. The first meal I cooked was to become his favourite, to be prepared over and over again in the happier times that followed. In retrospect, perhaps I should have given him the recipe as a parting gift.

Two years later we were married. Ours was one of the first marriages to be performed at Ashoka Hotel as my mother's sensibility could not accept the prospect of endless discussions with caterers, whom she called *halwai*s, the tent house people, or any other 'semi literate' persons. They, according to her, had no sense of hygiene and were loud and vulgar people. No end of arguments or circumstantial proof of other relatives' weddings could convince her that her fears were unfounded and only resided in her head. I was deeply mortified, as were some of my relatives. To add injury to insult, the *prasad,* a most eagerly awaited part of any Sikh religious ceremony, was not going to be cooked by the traditional priest of the gurudwara, chanting hymns from the Granth Sahib while doing so. Instead, it was going to be the handiwork of the newly acquired French chef of the hotel, who had accepted my mother's challenge like a true French chevalier, and indeed he cooked it to perfection. On the appointed day, the bride decided to listen to her inner voice which told her this was a mistake, that he was not the right man for her, and I eventually had to be persuaded to join the impatient bridegroom under the influence of three shots of Hennessey XO. I was beyond fashionably late and missed the drama of the head priest of Sis Ganj Gurudwara abdicating his responsibility to perform the marriage as the groom was a 'Mona Sikh', or one who has cut his hair and disobeyed the diktats of Guru Gobind Singh to honour the five visible signs of Sikhism.

Fortunately the enlightened gurus had stressed that anyone who could read the verses from the Granth Sahib which solemnized marriage in the presence of five witnesses could perform the Anand Karaj (Sikh wedding). I demurely sat down next to my Mona Sikh to be balefully glared at by his dragon aunt who served as our acting priest. If these were not early signs that all not quite well

Dr Harbans Dhillon performing our marriage, Delhi, 9th December, 1973.

with the state of the young Grewal marriage, the cherry on the cake was my father-in-law's suggestion that *he* should be sleeping at the India International Centre room which we had reserved for ourselves. He needed to get away from a household of relatives intently catching up on family gossip. His sensibility could not tolerate the noise pollution any longer as, according to him, his in-laws, good fun-loving people from Assam, had kept him awake all night with their singing and dancing.

The hero of my script metamorphosed very early in the marriage, revealing his determined anti-hero face. The script however also had within it a heroine whose impact would become palpable after many years. Throughout my childhood and adolescence I had longed for the comfort of a traditional upbringing where a father was the unquestionable authority as head of the family. Mother stayed home and cooked, and was always there to greet the children and her husband with a warm smile, surrounding everyone with her loving and self-sacrificing warmth. How desperate I to was to be 'normal'. This was not something I understood from friends' homes and their families (mine was distinctly out of the box). It was from the reel life heroines played by Meena Kumari and her ilk. The self-sacrificing mothers/wives/sisters/daughters were my role models. How I longed to slip into their skins, determined that when I got married I would not be the subject of any strife: the continual fantasy of most children who grow up in dysfunctional families: 'We are not going to be like that.' Desperate to begin their own adult lives independent of any residue of familial influences, but alas, most marry early and Act One begins.

Coming from an egalitarian/feudal background, a guaranteed 'to confuse' ingredient, I was shocked to see B ordering the domestic help to polish his shoes. The perfect cue for Meena Kumari, spurred on by a closet 'Hunterwali' to announce that 'I will polish his shoes.' The servant had no choice but I did. Why stop at that? After all, although I had moved away from all the influences of my parental home I did have an inbuilt propensity towards the excessive. I took on the complete role of the perfect valet. Laid out his clothes, cooked breakfast, packed delicious, innovative lunches, sometimes romantically slipping in a loving note. I served him his food on a plate, all aesthetically placed so that no two flavours merged, only to see him, the complete boarding school product, mix it all up. I can't remember whether I assisted him in taking off his shoes: no, I couldn't possibly have done that; at least I hope not. A perfect marriage. or so I imagined.

My friends, family, and other beings looked at me as if

I had been transformed into an alien beyond recognition. The oft-heard lament was 'Where are you? Who is this stranger?' I paid no heed, snug in the knowledge that I was living the ideal life. The contradiction in my flawed fantasy was that my Meena Kumari was not fond of alcohol: a key prop was missing. The cookie began to crumble.

After a brief failed experiment of living with his parents we moved into a barsati in Defence Colony. We bonded over creating a home together. As we were among the first of his friends to get married, our home became a club-house for all our friends. Evenings would be spent drinking rum, listening to music, talking books and films. Although living on a shoestring budget we felt privileged to live the lives we had chosen for ourselves. I recall this stage with great fondness, as in many ways we were like two infants in the woods playing house-house. It was during our barsati days that I was introduced to art movies by a dear friend who we thought became more alive in the reel world than in the real world. A's intensity while watching films was endearing and I would often be looking at him and his changing expressions rather than at the screen. That was especially so because some of the films he insisted we must see were so bleak and dark that I really needed a diversion to survive the two hours in the cinema hall. I once committed the cardinal error of asking for a packet of popcorn, and the unexpected reaction caught me completely off guard. I suddenly felt his hand gripping my throat as he hissed 'You don't eat popcorn when you are watching Sergei Eisenstein.'

The marriage however became larger than the two people who wished to build a life together. His mission was to follow in the steps of Peter Pan and mine to be the 'good wife'. He was more faithful to his hero, I a colossal failure. We did have our moments; memories that sustain a niggardly fondness for the man.

The years preceding 'The End' were happy ones or so I thought, although the scorpion's tail did sting at unexpected moments. We were however young and certain we would have our way. We were moreover confident in our cocooned idealism, sharing an unfettered belief that we could change the world into a more loving and gentle place. The personal was political and the political personal. Perhaps we stretched this point to its limits when having or adopting a baby became a topic of debate. This took place not just between the two of us, but within our circle of friends. The debate stretched to accommodate all points of view, including one that said 'the desire for progeny is the ultimate extension of one's ego. It matters little whether a child is adopted or born of you; the imprint is yours.' The central question: 'Why after seven years of marriage do you want a child?' was never really satisfactorily answered by either of us. Two potential pairs of grandparents despaired.

When did I start paying heed to my biological clock? The irrational desire to conceive. Buoyed up by weak arguments: 'Let me undergo the experience. Then I will be better prepared for an adopted child.' It smacked of my own unpreparedness: not wanting to be an instant parent. To get pregnant was to be allowed a gestation period towards parenthood. Instant conception was not very easy either. Thus began the 'am I barren' phase. What an ugly word. A patriarchical notion that has kept woman shackled from biblical Sara and Ruth to me. How could I, a feminist, equate womanhood with motherhood? A woman is complete in herself; she does not need to be a mother.

No, I could not be consoled with rationality. I wanted a baby: my very own baby. The obsession spread to friends, my colleagues in Saheli. My life was punctuated by a single question: is she or is she not? That was until 'she is' was uttered and there was a community hurrah. Also, a much-relieved B, who had experienced his wife metamorphosing into an alien creature. We could all reclaim our lives, except that mine turned into a series of unfamiliar experiences.

I experienced the special sensuality of pregnancy, secretly celebrating a sense of 'completeness' I had not felt earlier. I would stand naked in front of the mirror, looking at myself from all angles, admiring my roundness, and feeling so special. I loved the languid sensuality of every gesture. The life within was not independent of me: we shared a private conversation to which no one else was privy. I felt surreal being amongst all the people I loved, and as if a part of me had moved away to map new paths. Everything seemed to lead to an inward journey. Discussions, conversations, concerns which till a short while earlier had been the most central issues in my life suddenly diffused into distractions. I suddenly metamorphosed into an island, building a safe refuge for the life within. It made me want to reach out to all the pregnant women I saw, shocked at how commonplace the 'sightings' were. So many, many pregnant women.

The rational feminist side of me proclaimed that there was more to life than being pregnant, so get on with it and reclaim your real life. This was what I did, secure in the knowledge that yes, there was another way of being; accepting all the attention and fuss as my due.

Nikhat was the much awaited baby of all my friends as many of them had bade farewell to baby-rearing days and were preoccupied with children's homework, tantrums, and all the essentials required of a 'good' mother. The evening of Nikhat's birth my hospital room resembled a mini pub with all my friends in a happy state of being. Such a sight did not amuse the gynaecologist on her rounds who shooed them all out of the hospital. Fortunately Nikhat was safe in the nursery wing of the hospital. I realized that I did not possess the two essential perquisites of being a good mother: enjoying breastfeeding and making strange baby sounds. These, I was informed, were essential for mother-child bonding. The first I managed for three months, the second I substituted by reading aloud to her anything I happened to reading. She gurgled, hiccupped, frowned, made funny and sorrowful faces throughout my reading to her of Salman Rushdie's *Midnight Children* from the proof copy I was given by a friend at Penguin. This had been his practice for many years: to hand me proof copies and seek my opinion before ordering the quantities he expected to sell. In this, through a curious twist of intuition, I had not disappointed him. I am convinced that Nikhat's advanced vocabulary and uttering complete sentences at 11 months was a direct result of that. She never learnt to sit, walked at 12 months, cut her first tooth at 13 months, and she talked and talked and talked, and identified all the Rafters from Salim Ali's *Common Birds of India*.

School admissions were not the herculean, tension-ridden experience they are today. Nikhat spent her first couple of years in Magic Years, a Montessori nursery in which today parents will go to great lengths to get their children admitted. Then onwards to Sardar Patel Vidyalaya, another of those schools. All my peers had their children at SPV which had its inverted snob profile of being focused on teaching good Hindi to the children. We experienced at first-hand how contrary parents were, as we, who could not sustain a conversation in Hindi, wanted our daughter to do so. Well, SPV was the In school

Nikhat in my arms, Delhi, 1984.

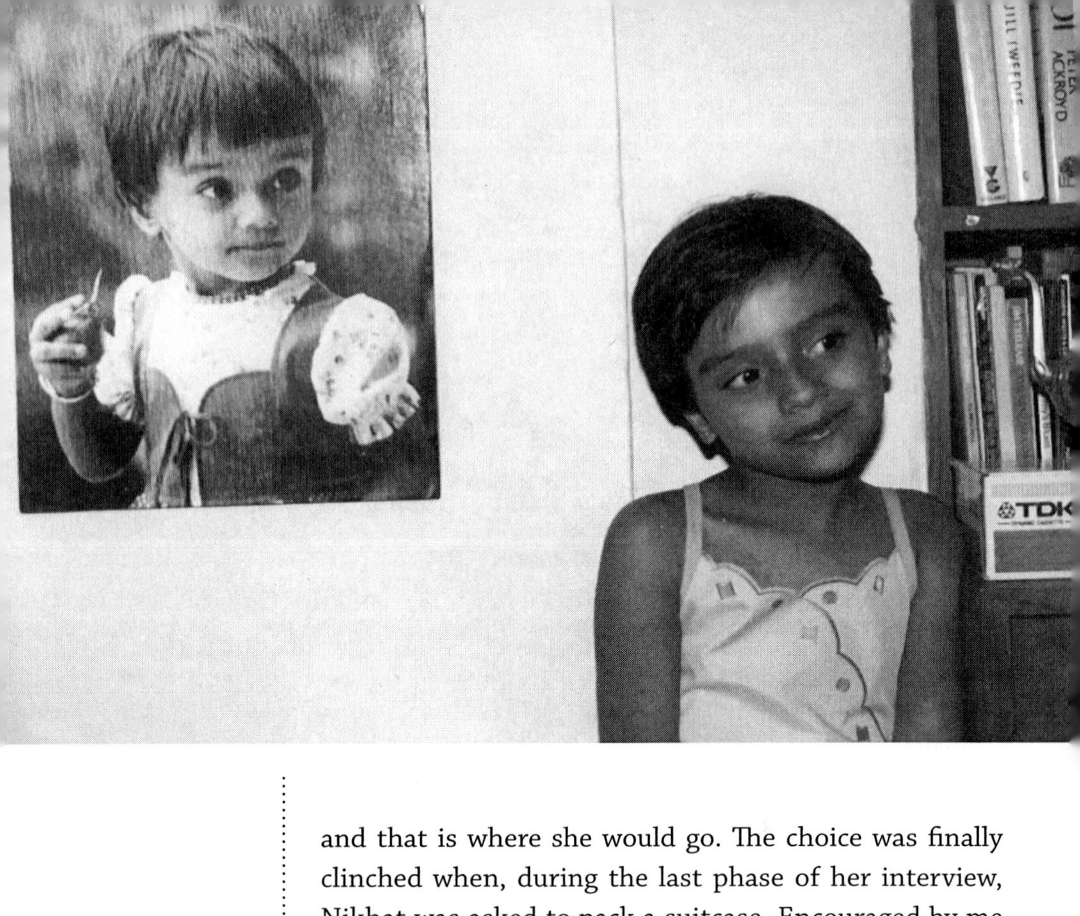

Vignettes of Nikhat, Delhi, 1982 and 1985.

and that is where she would go. The choice was finally clinched when, during the last phase of her interview, Nikhat was asked to pack a suitcase. Encouraged by me to pack a suitcase for her father which she had seen me do many times, she circled all the essentials thrice, then picked up three glasses and placed them in the suitcase and shut it. When questioned on her choice of essentials, my daughter primly replied in Hindi, ‘Yes that is what my Papa needs: one glass each for morning, afternoon, and evening drink.’ The silence in the room could be cut with a knife. We went home despondent that this was it: no chance. To our astonishment and delight we received an admission letter. The school we believed was on a mission of redemption.

School closing time was crowded with a gaggle of friends and acquaintances all waiting to collect their children. We could have opened a mini bar at the parking lot. Our separation years later caused my first disillusionment with the school: at their lack of sensitivity, when some some of the teachers took the moral high ground. The scales tipped when Nikhat was asked by her teacher to write a short (six sentences) essay on Diwali. She wrote that she would ‘burst many crackers and eat mutton biryani’ to celebrate Diwali, and ended it with *shukria*. Her page was red-inked with a caustic remark that on Diwali all good Indians perform puja and eat vegetarian food; also, *shukria* is not a Hindi word, use *dhanyavad*.

Enough. The child really needed to go to a regular school. Nikhat was caught between her parents' passion for jungles and birds, and her mother at regular intervals inviting in women in need of interim shelter. To cap it was Nikhat's own pain and bewilderment at her father remaining away from home for extended periods. Life for this young 11 year child was becoming crowded with 'politically correct' preciousness. The choice of school? Lawrence School Sanawar. It was a change from chalk to

Nikhat, wearing a medal won at an equestrian meet, 1995.

With Nikhat (Courtesy: Dayanita Singh).

cheese. After the initial six months of ‘her nose is always red’, as my godson informed me, Nikhat never looked back, and grew into a lovely, strong, caring, and bright young woman.

I did receive a letter from the principal of SPV when we withdrew Nikhat, emphasizing my poor parenting in pulling her out of the school and denying her a holistic, superior education, also adding that she would never be readmitted.

- 12 -

The Emergency

We begin playing the game 'What if' very early in life. These two loaded words spark our imagination, and our favoured endings. What if the sky falls? What if he had just left five minutes later and then he would not have been struck by a truck and died. What if I had not ventured out and been able to attend to my uncle's heart attack? What if Mahatma Gandhi had known of Jinnah's terminal illness and then appointed him prime minister of undivided India? Sadly, when the question is asked in the context of history it echoes back clouded with regrets; a sense that things could have taken a far more propitious turn.

Indira Gandhi's decision to get President Fakhruddin Ahmed, who was like putty in her hands, to declare a state of national emergency, was a 'What if' moment. What if this enormously popular heroine of the 1971 war, who had won a decisive election, a military victory in a short space of a year, had not done so. The people of India who cherish their gods and even more their goddesses had installed her on a high worshipful pedestal. What if she had not forgotten that 'all power corrupts and absolute power corrupts absolutely'? What if she had continued in the footsteps of her father and supported collective leadership and internal democracy within the Congress party? What if she had not metamophosed slowly and surely transformed into a ruthless, autocratic prime minister.

What too if she had not allowed her younger son Sanjay Gandhi to influence her and quashed his ambitious plan to set up a plant to manufacture 'the first wholly Indian-built car': Maruti, son of the wind god. Who was he, other than her much beloved son? None other than a brash, opinionated dropout apprentice with Rolls Royce with extremely limited skills and analytical abilities.

The Maruti project from its inception was dogged by controversies; accused of nepotism. Questions were raised about Sanjay's lack of expertise and experience, the acquisition of prime land on the outskirts of Delhi.

For the first time in parliament there were continuing disruptions on allegations of corruption that were lapped up by the press. What if he had succeeded in manufacturing the car completely indigenously, and not relied on Suzuki, a Japanese automobile manufacturer, to salvage the project ?

The first 10,000 cars were imported from Japan. By 1974 the Maruti controversy and high inflation, real or perceived corruption charges against Sanjay Gandhi, and osmotically his mother, had become the catalyst

Indira Gandhi and Zail Singh with Sanjay Gandhi (Courtesy: Hindustan Times).

Jayaprakash Narayan addressing the Boat Club rally (Courtesy: Hindustan Times).

for mass agitations against the prime minister who had been lionized by the people of India.

What if Jayaprakash Narayan, a veteran nationalist, much respected and regarded as Mahatma Gandhi's moral heir, had not called for non-violent civil disobedience to bring down the government?.

What if India's economy had been stronger?

What if George Fernandes, a young trade union leader, had not led the railway workers to launch a national strike in 1974, paralysing the country and preventing even the most essential commodities from reaching the people through India's lifeline, the railways?

What if she had decided to negotiate with the workers on the advice of her railway minister and chairman of the railway board as the strike was essentially on simple economic issues? She however viewed it as a political challenge to her leadership.

What if she had not ruthlessly quelled the railway workers' strike, an action seen by many young idealist leaders of the JP movement as a precursor to an emergent fascist government?

What if Indira Gandhi had restrained herself from courting the image of a decisive leader by encouraging her nuclear scientists to test explode a nuclear device: ironically code-named 'Smiling Buddha'?

What if she had honoured the Allahabad High Court judgement indicting her of electoral malpractice and resigned with grace and honour?

And finally, what if she had resisted her son's and some of her cronies' advice to declare a state of Emergency?

The Emergency was declared, leaders of the

opposition and other dissenting voices were jailed. These included students of Jawaharlal Nehru University (viewed as the radical left), social activists working with daily wage farm labour in Mehrauli, and anyone else who she, or more often her son, believed were a threat to their continuance in power. The fourth estate was completely and ruthlessly muzzled. Unfortunately only two national dailies had the spine and moral compass to stand tall as members of the free press, the rest succumbing to Sanjay's diktats.

Initially a large number of Indians (who are largely apolitical), were welcoming of the Emergency, as trains and buses for once ran on schedule and the prices of vegetable and other essential commodities fell markedly. Bureaucrats were seen arriving on time and actually working in their offices. Sanjay Gandhi reigned supreme as did his handpicked deputies, some of whom, much later, found their way back to Rajiv's government. The police basked in the acquisition of virtually unlimited power, 'taking care' of personal enmities and muzzling all dissentient voices. The judiciary bent, as did other autonomous and semi-autonomous institutions, while holding their heads high and proclaiming their nonpartisan credentials. Sycophancy within the Congress and bureaucracy reached such heights that it became an impossible task for most to touch rational terra firma ever again. So much was destroyed in so short a time.

We felt as though the world around us had suddenly turned a murky shade of grey, denied the freedom to ever breathe fresh clean air again. Our brave attempt at cyclostyling anti-emergency leaflets and surreptitiously pasting them on walls was no real consolation. We knew we were impotent and all our efforts would actually make no difference whatsoever. I awoke every morning

Sanjay addressing a public rally, Delhi, 1975 (Courtesy: PIB).

feeling choked. Delhi reminded me of Saddam Hussein's Baghdad. The sickening stories of mass sterilizations, of men being forcibly rounded up, bundled into trucks, and taken away to be vasectomized, was redolent of Hitler's Germany. Targets had to be met and exceeded. Adolescents, young unmarried men, old men, priests, anyone and everyone was rounded up and herded away.

The first mass protest in the country was launched in Amritsar as the 'Campaign to Save Democracy'. It was organized by the Akali Dal and stated: 'The question before us is not whether Indira Gandhi should continue to be prime minster or not. The point is whether democracy in this country is to survive or not.' It goes without saying that all protestors during the 20 months of the Emergency were arrested without trial; of these, according to some records, 40,000 came from India's two per cent Sikh minority.

Innumerable books, plays, and films have been written and produced in the aftermath of the Emergency, a telling commentary on the enormity of this dark phase in India's history and how deeply it affected the collective conscience. Rahi Masoom Raza's *Qatra Bi Arzoo*, Rohinton Mistry's *Such a Long Journey*, *Midnight's*

Children by Salman Rushdie, and several regional novels all portray the blatant misuse of power and infringement of individual freedoms. Gulzar's *Aandhi* was banned because it was supposedly based on Indira Gandhi as was Amrit Nahata's *Kissa Kursi Ka,* and I.S. Johar's *Nasbandi* openly criticizing the excesses of the Emergency. The list is long.

The collective memory of that shameful and horrific period long haunted us. While campaigning for a friend during Rajiv Gandhi's first election there would be a mass exodus of young men, women carrying their babies, and children following them into the fields to hide. Puzzled by this very curious behaviour, I decided to dig deeper and was directed towards the 'Calcutta ladies'. Well-meaning friends of the future member of parliament had in their wisdom decided on full-sleeved blouses and white sarees with dark borders as their election 'costume'. The young men would take one look at them and run for their lives shouting '*nasbandi*', while the women would be clutching the babies screaming '*teeka wali*'.

One last thought: What if Indira Gandhi had not called for elections on 23 January 1977? Mercifully she did, and we, with hundreds of Dilliwallahs, danced on the streets of Bahadurshah Zafar Marg to celebrate her defeat and looked expectantly ahead to a new beginning with 'Our Janata Party'.

- 13 -

Growth of Civil Liberty and Women's Organizations

Delhi is a city that lives at many subterranean levels. My memories are just as complex, each experience flowing into another, churning into a composite whole and enriching my life.

One of the few positive fallouts of the Emergency was the birth of many civil liberty groups throughout India. Informal meetings were regularly organized by individuals and groups under the broad umbrella of PUCLDR (People's Union for Civil Liberties and Democratic Rights). The discussions revolved around the political ramifications of the Emergency on the lives of the general public, and the consequences of the enactment of draconian laws like MISA which enabled an ordinary citizen to be arrested and detained on mere suspicion. They encapsulated the effect of the underlying fear psychosis among the common man arising from the regime of forced sterilization and censorship of the print media.

Veteran leader Jayaprakash Narayan (JP) had founded the PUCLDR pre-Emergency in 1976. Many who had worked with him were subsequently inducted as cabinet ministers in the Janata Party in April 1977. The People's Union for Civil Liberty (PUCL) was formed as an organization free from political ideology to enable people from various political persuasions to share a common platform focusing on the defence of civil liberties and human rights. Beginning with this period, the discourse on non-governmental initiatives and organizations underwent a sea change. At one end of the spectrum was a tendency that identified itself both with the national movement and the struggles faced by those who opposed the Emergency. At the other end, there was a strong belief that the formulation of the 1950s and '60s, namely, of viewing non-governmental organizations as links between government and people in the process of planning and development, should be revived.

This period between the late 1960s to the early '80s saw the growth of several voluntary organizations, more appropriately called Social Action Groups, in response to the rising frustration with existing approaches and models of development and their ineffectiveness in solving the problems of poverty, unemployment, and similar issues. It was an exciting period when new movements were taking root. Thousands of young people outside the formal framework of party politics and the government initiated activities relating to the rural and urban poor. To the earlier concerns of poverty, inequality, and eradication of social injustices were now added issues of gender, environment, human rights (land entitlement, minimum wages, the liberation of bonded labour). These movements fearlessly combated the local power-centres, such as forest contractors (as in the Chipko movement), and engaged in mass agitations against the state (as in the construction of large dams (the Silent Valley and Sardar Sarovar projects). 'Struggles' and 'movements' for organizing the poor, 'conscientization', and 'people's empowerment' became catchwords for social activists. Politics once again became central to activism. The non-governmental sector began being viewed and assessed in terms of its efficacy in promoting new issues, in helping to organize the poor more effectively, and developing a new framework of rights and entitlements.

The work began to encompass issues and campaigns relating to drought, floods, deforestation, environment, land alienation, bonded labour, housing rights, water, pollution, and the like. All these required a degree of professional expertise, whether technical, legal, administrative, or other. Added to this was the accent on women, particularly as the issue was raised by the nascent women's movement in India and partly as a result of the now very vocal international movement for women's rights. Women's issues now became integral to all NGO activities.

•

Action India was founded in 1976 and began its work with clusters of displaced Bengalis who had migrated to Delhi for a better life. Most of them came from Midnapur on the border of Bangladesh and we suspected that among them were Bangladesh migrants as a spillover from the liberation of East Pakistan. I was never able to comprehend why the birth of a new nation invariably witnessed mass emigration of legitimate citizens of a certain class and religious background. We could sense the pain, conflict, and aspirations of this community, many of whom were rickshaw-pullers who had come to Delhi hoping for a miracle but were living as the forgotten people of yet another illegal slum. Not many facilities were provided and the majority of their children were reduced to becoming rag-pickers to provide meagre support to their families. Our objectives in Action India of working with them was to make them aware of their constitutional rights. To help them to learn how to strategize their strengths, and serve as an interface with government officials. These officials more often than not had either failed to meet them despite confirmed appointments or hastily made empty promises, doubtless to get them quickly out their offices and with them the unwashed odour that clung like a second skin. Just how fragile their tenements were became patently obvious to them and us when the chairman of the DDA, Jagmohan, who had the grandiose vision of recreating the magnificence of what had been Shahjanabad, took advantage of the Emergency and bulldozed their homes, destroying, along with their meagre belongings, the few memories of the home and childhood they had left behind. All were decimated beneath the might of the state, with a carte blanche from Sanjay Gandhi, no notice or explanation being deemed to be necessary.

The closest we got to an explanation was when we asked Jagmohan why the people who had lived there had been heartlessly divided as a community, some of them having been relocated to New Seemapuri to build new homes on 25 sq yd plots, with a miserly government payout, while the other half were despatched to Jehangirpuri under the same conditions. He explained that it was government strategy to divide the minority communities, as a large cluster could become a problem in the future. How well we had learnt from our British masters: Divide and Rule.

The travesty of establishing resettlement (*jhuggi-jhonpri* [JJ]) colonies would have led to strong anti-government protests/dharnas, but for the law prohibiting the assembly of over four persons. The poor 'resettled' people could not afford one extra day of being laid off from work and perforce accepted their new grim resettlement housing. The JJ colonies had no sewage or drainage facilities, and the common toilets were forever clogged with light bulbs being continually pilfered, making them unsafe for women to use after nightfall. The new inhabitants were resented by the earlier settlers, largely from Uttar Pradesh and Rajasthan, who viewed with suspicion and disdain. Their workplaces were miles away, public transport biting into their meagre earnings. This was the vision of New India drafted by Nehru's grandson under his 20 Point Programme, a far cry from the Nehruvian vision of just one and a half decades earlier. This was yet another face of my Delhi that was teaching me lessons on what it feels like to be so disenfranchised as human beings. Barely had the people become familiar with their new habitation than, ever so often, the unquiet silence would be disturbed by a roll of drums and clang of cymbals to herald Sanjay Gandhi's women groupies. Clad in *ghagra*s and dancing to the music, they would encourage all the men, young and old, to come to the sterilization camps, promising cash and other incentives. Notwithstanding our rage and disgust we could not help being amused by these 'society ladies' dancing for the slummy unwashed of the world. Sanjay Gandhi certainly seemed to have the knack of bringing out the absurd and the comic amongst his adherents, besides, of course, winning their loyalty. Some of the men in the communities agreed to sterilization only for the small cash envelope they received after the vasectomy. This was hubris at its best: first the state displaces them, then offers them 'lollipops' in exchange for additional numbers in its target game.

During that period I did meet Mr Chairman of the Delhi Development Authority (DDA), floating high on the power of the bulldozer, at a friend's house for dinner. I confronted him on why he had focused on the poor illegal occupants of government land rather than all the wealthy Maharani Bagh and Friends Colony owners who had appropriated pavements within the boundaries of their plots. Surprisingly, my words had some effect, because the very next evening he called me triumphantly to report that he had had all the 'élite' boundary walls torn down. The Bulldozer had once again reigned supreme.

Our group would hold all manner of meetings, from planning covert distribution of anti-Emergency leaflets, to trying to answer the larger questions of equity and the right to housing, drinking water, and education enshrined in our constitution. Some of the members tried flirting with the larger Naxalite movement. All of them found me just a trifle bizarre because I never ceased to wear the gold anklets my mother had given me, even when visiting highly impoverished areas, questioning my insensitivity. As I saw it, it would have been insensitive to pretend that I was one person in the slums meeting those who had opened up their hearts and homes to us, and a different one when living the upper middle-class life I led beyond their world. I accepted the JJ colony dwellers as they were, and they reciprocated, sometimes even wondering why some of my companions dressed so shabbily when they visited the *basti*.

As a group we eventually forged individual friendships, which are as strong today as it was in those days when we sat with our pegs of rum in the evenings listening to and dancing to music. Our favourites, Simon & Garfunkel, The Beatles, Joan Baez, and as the evening slipped into early morning, the velvet voices of Frank Sinatra and Nat King Cole. These melodious voices would act as a balm to our sinking thoughts about the inevitability of economic disparity between Indians, the unnecessary deaths of their babies, endemic tuberculosis amongst the men who, notwithstanding this, had perforce to continue the arduous task of plying their cycle-rickshaws .... There was however also the pleasure derived from nurturing potential leadership among some of them, especially the women. Some of us decided to work with those in the other blocks as a strategy to bring them all on a common platform to demand better services from the government and the politicians who visited them just prior to elections. Each small success was celebrated as a major victory.

Then came a fateful day when a short-circuit in one of the 'stolen' electric wires burnt 67 *jhuggi*es to cinder. We sat on a mound with the residents, impotently witnessing once again the destruction of the little they possessed. A donor offered monetary assistance but we as a group, after a long debate on the politics of funding, decided to reject the offer. Our error lay in not including the community leaders in our discussion, and that led to great animosity. This was because those affected were in such urgent need of assistance that they were in no position to wait for the distant day when the government might pay their dues. We were unceremoniously kicked out, a five-year relationship unable to withstand the power of money. It was a hard lesson for all of us from the privileged class.

•

As political news, or any other relevant news that might be deemed to be anti-government, or more particularly anti-Indira-Sanjay Gandhi was effectively censored, newspapers that had not voluntarily shut office, began reporting non-confrontational social news, and for the first time dowry deaths became front page headlines. A group of us had already begun meeting prior to the Emergency to discuss the feminist movement which was changing the polity in the West and its relevance to women in India. We called our group Stree Sangarsh and met once a week. Initially it was almost like a book club where we deliberated the writings of Germaine Greer, Betty Freidan, Susan Sontag, Paulo Freire, Adrienne Rich and Maya Angelou. We also discussed the role of Clara Zetkin in the Marxist movement and her influence on Lenin. Gradually there began a debate closer to home as the battle of Western feminists on issues such as abortion did not directly affect us. We focused on the right to safe abortions, to own our bodies, to plan our families, effective redressal against violence, to choose to study rather than become victim to an early arranged marriage, and the right to a safe work environment. Almost all the members of our group were from the privileged class, and although we did experience certain male biases, we were certainly not subjected to the conventional strictures of the form of patriarchal society prevalent in the slums in which we worked. Into this group, which was more a platform for intellectual discourse to broaden our own understanding of the deep-rooted gender biases, dowry deaths intruded like a rude shock. The very idea of a wife being actually burnt to death by her husband and in-laws because she could not fulfil their rapacious material demands was just too horrifying to contemplate.

Dowry deaths then began dominating all our meetings till we read about another horrible 'murder' in Punjabi Bagh, where once again the police had refused to file an FIR and all evidence had been destroyed. Stree Sangarsh, along with other like-minded organizations, including members from PUCLDR, took out its first anti-dowry demonstration and formed a picket outside the site of the crime. It was an exhilarating moment, and especially so because many people from the neighbourhood joined us and the newspapers covered it. This was the beginning of the first public debate on dowry deaths, and the apathetic attitude of law enforcement agencies which were staffed by men and women who were themselves either victims or culprits of dowry demands and domestic violence. One such was Satya Rani Chadha whose daughter had been burnt by her husband and in-laws. She had over the years became a strong advocate

Satyarani Chadha with a photograph of her daughter who was burnt to death for dowry. Satyarani became an activist fighting against domestic violence and set up her own organization to campaign for justice (Courtesy: Sheba Chhachhi).

of women's rights, the anti-dowry movement, and had helped countless women in the 'cow belt' to escape unimaginable oppression and also retrieve their dowries. She eventually received justice from the Indian judicial system after appearing in courts for almost 30 years and on each occasion leaving disappointed. Some of us took

turns to accompany her to court. I usually returned in a blazing temper after having spent almost the entire day rubbing shoulders with corrupt policemen, insensitive lawyers, and indifferent judges, many of them absenting themselves after lunch.

We realized that for many, dowry harassment and violence against women were an accepted given. How then could we change this attitude in which society itself was complicit? We were devastated to think that this was happening in the capital of the largest democracy in the world, and in a country proud of its Constitution which enshrined justice for all with special emphasis on the vulnerable sections of society. We agonized ceaselessly on the causes, concluding that the fundamental reasons for the devaluation of young women's lives were the changing profiles of society post-1947, rising consumerism and aspirations, lack of easy bank credit, and other such issues.

We decided that to explore the subject more fully and also to spread wider awareness of the issue, we should take it to the streets. *Om Swaha*, a play on dowry, was written after several months of discussions and the assistance of friends Maya Rao and Anuradha Kapoor from the

As founder member of Theatre Union, a street theatre group formed in 1979, Maya Rao collaborated to make and perform, "Om Swaha" (on dowry, 1979). It went on to become a popular play with various womens' and other groups, and was translated and performed in several languages all over India.

theatre world. Most of the play was conceptualized on the lawns of a friend's house whose father was a member of parliament. The irony of discussing issues that questioned the state from the residence of an MP only vetted our theatrical talents. Over the next few months we walked the streets of Delhi setting up stage wherever we could, generating a mixed response, both supportive and hostile. Since its debut, *Om Swaha* has been used on innumerable occasions as a powerful tool to bring not only the dowry issue but other crimes against women to the attention of the general public as well as of students in colleges and schools. It has served as a catalyst to generate meaningful discussions by more groups than we could have ever dreamt, particularly in rural north India.

•

The Saheli Women's Resource Centre was set up in 1980 with members of the same 'bourgeois' group as a vehicle to help people who had either directly faced violent or discriminatory acts or whose family members had been subjected to them. It was intended as an organization with a formal forum where a larger group of both women and a men could meet over the weekends to discuss and frame strategies concerning civil society. The aim was to exert public pressure on the government and parliamentarians to introduce remedial measures that would protect the rights of all citizens and ensure that in future no revocation of human freedoms could arise. The group consisted of activists who worked in organizations engaged in raising the consciousness of the poor by helping them organize themselves to demand their basic rights. Those involved included people from the state and central governments, lawyers working on human rights issues, journalists, judges, and a small group of social scientists. The legal amendments we proposed related to dowry, rape, and other gender inequities. Saheli was never intended to become a crisis centre. The crisis aspect, that is, working with individual women, just developed as an offshoot.

Saheli was initially begun by nine women in the garage of one of Saheli's founder-members in No. 10 Nizamuddin East. We had a corpus of Rs 80, a broom, bucket, dusters (the latter three were my contributions as feminists in the early 1980s did not pay much attention in keeping the work place spick and span or preetifying themselves; these being viewed as patriarchal shackles.) Our furniture, typewriter, and other 'office equipment' were donated. We were as proud of our collective space as any young married couple would have been in their first personal apartment. The place felt secure and one in which each of us could drop our guard and really learn about ourselves as individuals. We maintained a Daily Diary for the first 10 years because most members came in as volunteers for short periods during the day and had to keep the next Saheli worker informed about any visits, etc., prior to her arrival. The Daily Diary soon became for us a personal communications platform. It also served as a vehicle for comment on the negative traits we noticed in one another. This was a convenient form of mutual criticism, rather than having face-offs over generally trivial issues but which were sufficiently important for healthy group dynamics. Mine usually centred on what the rest termed or sneered at as the *jharu-pochha* variety'.

There was no formal announcement of our existence, just word of mouth. Within days of opening our walk-in centre, we received all manner of visitors. Some were curious passersby who eventually returned with someone who needed help. Some came because they thought we were a tailoring unit or a beauty parlour. Others just dropped in for a chat and cup of tea, like the two eunuchs who visited us regularly and made us privy to their stories. (Many years later I woke up to a frantic ringing of the doorbell of my newly redeveloped flat to see two familiar faces who had come not for tea but on a professional visit. My three large dogs wagged their tails to the rhythm of their clapping. They extracted all that was in my wallet: a couple of thousand rupees. They then blessed the house and promised to pay me a more personal visit, and so they did, and we had a good laugh and chit-chat over samosas and hot tea.)

At Saheli we were very clear that we were a collective and there would never be a hierarchy among us. This remained one of the central guiding principles which members of Saheli hold sacred to this day. Another principle was to never accept foreign funds because it would be unethical and smack of neo-colonialism to fight our government, judiciary, and law-enforcement agencies with foreign funding. That is a debate that continues to this day among other such organizations, albeit among a much smaller group working at the grass roots.

The garage of No. 10 Nizamuddin East soon became a hotbed of controversy. We were not formally equipped to counsel individual women who came to us as none of us had a degree in counselling or psychology . In the early months we just listened to the horror-stories of repeated physical and mental assaults, not just by husbands but also the in-laws. We heard from young girls that they had been pressurized into conforming to the diktats of male relatives, or of their rejection from natal homes. Of their being made to feel that it was always the woman's fault, of the helplessness of knowing they had no support from anyone. The established counselling centres were entirely garbed in a patriarchal value system espousing societal notions of the 'good wife'. We had no experience in handling cases of incest because it took us a long time to understand and accept that a young girl could be subjected to such a violation. Most of us believed that incest happened only in Greek tragedies.

It all began within months of opening the doors of the garage. A young woman came to us for help. When she came again, we counselled her that if she left home it didn't mean freedom (a piece of advice we gave every young woman). That it in fact implied less freedom because freedom means that at every level you are responsible for yourself. Therefore, in order to protect yourself you must think it over very carefully; your principles must be very strong. She eventually opened her heart to us and spoke about being sexually abused by her brother. Suddenly, to an invisible cue, her parents and brother barged in with the Nizamuddin police and accused us of having kidnapped the girl. Another *saheli,* Gita Sahgal and I were marched to the police station along with a young reporter from *Indian Express*, Sanjay Suri, who had come to interview us. His crime? Questioning the police. They put us in the lock-up, while the girl was dragged kicking and screaming home by her brother and father. No-one in those days had cellphones. The reporter was allowed just one phone call and, because he was a journalist, was able to ring up a couple of people. With his assistance we were also allowed one phone call to another *saheli* who spent the next 45 minutes calling all the associate members for support. That's the first time we realized that we counted for nothing in the larger state machinery which could revoke individual rights, even post-Emergency, on the basis of devious technical lacunae.

We were interrogated like common felons. There were no policewoman present, and none of our connections to the celebrated and the powerful proved a deterrent. During the four hours of custodial detention we began realizing that we were on the receiving end of class and gender hostility. The police were aware that our connections would get us out of their power sooner than they might have wished, so the purpose was to subject us to verbal 'third degree' and then plead ignorance to their superiors. We also realized that our status and class were actually working against us, although the less privileged were subjected to far worse treatment with no confidence that they would ever be freed from unlawful confinement. We saw the dehumanized face of our police force, but came out of the police lock-up to a hero's welcome from our network of human rights and voluntary groups, and academic friends. The Nizamuddin police was in a state of shock when they witnessed the active alliance and felt they had unwittingly disturbed a hornet's nest. The three detainees walked out six feet tall.

That incident made us the czarinas of women's rights and thenceforth no bureaucrat's or politician's door was closed in our faces. We could have been the precursors of the Gulabi Gang. It revealed the solidarity of all women's organizations and civil liberty groups which subsequently rose as one in the rousing protest over the Mathura episode. In that, a 16 year old tribal girl, Mathura, had been wrongfully detained and raped in custody by two police constables. In hindsight, the lack of interest and support of any political party (apart from Janwadi, the Marxist women's wing) for Mathura proved a blessing. It gave the campaign to protect women in custody and to amend the rape act an honest and vigorous voice involving no vested interests. It also encouraged the form of activism of many small women's and human right organizations in smaller cities and districts.

The blueprint was defined and strategies finely honed to challenge archaic laws and police corruption, and raise the bar on debates on domestic violence and equity. It also focused on the travails of the women's labour force in the unorganized garment sector, construction, and agriculture. By the end of Saheli's first year, from a sense of inadequacy and being overwhelmed we became much more conversant with legal procedures. Our methods of counselling seemed to be working as we were successfully persuading a few parents not to send their daughters back to their marital homes where they had been subjected to domestic violence. We also sent invitations on the five rupee yellow postcard to the husbands, and surprisingly 99 per cent of them came to us, bewildered at their wives having left them. For most, violence, both verbal and physical, was a way of life, they themselves having witnessed their mothers being subjected to the same treatment by their fathers and grandmothers.

After many weeks of counselling, for many couples, whenever reconciliation was achieved, it was a time of celebration because most of the women were in no position to become economically self-sufficient. A long list of mutually acceptable conditions would be set out on Saheli's letterhead and signed by the couple with Saheli members signing as witnesses. Today it is difficult to believe that this simple document was deemed to be legal and in most cases acted as a deterrent to the husband and his family.

The issue of incest, as noted above, came as an utter shock, and in particular the fact that it was quite a common aberration. We had to counsel young girls who had been raped by their fathers and brothers, with the mother reluctantly complicit in the crime, given that she had no alternative. To eradicate that deeply etched sense of shame was the most difficult part of the support we provided to individuals. Fortunately, a few years later, after innumerable discussions on incest, one young woman, part of the Saheli's outer circle, had the courage to step out and begin a crisis centre for girls and women with histories of family sexual abuse. The next most vulnerable group were pregnant schoolgirls who just walked into our premises in their school uniforms. We were fortunate that the Marie Stopes clinics had already opened and we were able to help them safely abort, but the degree of vulnerability of the female body — young, old, married, unmarried — was for us yet another eye-opener.

Then one day, in walked a very attractive educated young girl and her equally attractive, educated, caring, and protective boyfriend. We were all charmed by the young couple and for the first 10 minutes could not fathom whether they had come to become members of our extended group of supporters or something else. The story unfolded that they were in love and wanted to marry. She was Hindu and he a Muslim, and both faced stiff opposition from their families. Conversion to the other's religion was not an option they wished to exercise and had applied in Tees Hazari to be married under the Special Marriage Act. Unfortunately for them, this bastion of justice, upholder of the constitutional rights of all individuals, was vulnerable to a group of Hindu fundamentalists from the Vishwa Hindu Parishad (VHP). They visited the court each month to record inter-caste/religious marriages on the list posted outside the courtroom. The posting of this list was a necessary procedure, similar to the Christian banns, so that objections, if any, could be raised and taken cognizance of by the magistrate. The girl's family was visited by the president of the VHP, Ashok Singhal, himself, and the couple went 'underground' because the prospective groom feared for his life. Both the VHP and Ashok Singhal were alien names to us at Saheli as not many of us came from families who practised institutional religion, beyond a few token social rituals on Diwali, Eid, Christmas, and Guru Nanak's birthday. Who were these people, and why were they permitted to exert their muscle 37 years into independent India?

We did our utmost to support the court marriage of the young couple in the face of the pressure exerted by their families, and in particular by Ashok Singhal and his followers. They actually paid us a visit at Saheli with the parents and quietly, almost sweetly and in an avuncular tone informed us that 'this could never happen'. It was a challenge that we in Saheli accepted. Subsequently I received an anonymous call which informed me that they knew where I lived, and the bus stop where my daughter, all of 7 years, waited to catch her school bus. That if we involved ourselves in blemishing one of their daughters they would do the same to mine. Fortunately this was Delhi in the 1980s and not 2014–2015, so it remained just a background menace.

Today, thanks to all the struggles of our mothers and grandmothers who first drew attention to the woman's voice, which was stifled when the country shuddered into two, we have been able to protect that voice. Now it can be heard loud and clear, breaking out of the patriarchal bonds that traditionally defined what a woman should be. Today I can celebrate my confident, fearless 35 year old daughter, one among millions of young Indian women who take pride in their independence, courage,

An anti-dowry demonstration, Delhi, 1990s (Courtesy: Sheba Chhachhi).

and self-worth.

The young couple's story, however, ended in a truncated conversation and a traditional marriage as their car ride to the courts with us on the appointed day degenerated into a real-life Bollywood car chase. Our fragile Maruti 800, escorted by sympathetic supporters in a much weathered Ambassador, was completely hemmed in by giants from the VHP *akhara* in jeeps, who kept hurling strings of abuses at us until a police van intervened and stopped them for 'rash and negligent driving'. In all my Saheli days I can recall just one inter-religious civil wedding, when a friendly magistrate came to the residence of one of the *saheli*s.

Our youth, optimism, idealism, and above all, complete faith in our judicial system propelled us at every stage to commit our lives to fighting for justice. We were able to push through amendments in existing dowry legislation and ensure in-camera trials for rape victims. We rejoiced at the changes in the inheritance law which decreed equal inheritance for sons and daughters, albeit sparking a rift in many brother and sister relationships, particularly in Punjab. We, however, just shrugged these off as collateral damage.

Closer to home, my experience with domestic violence became a personal reality. My younger brother's wife filed a police complaint against my brother, father, and also my mother who was no more, for physical and verbal abuse under section 498A of the IPC. This was an Act for the which we and other women's groups in Delhi had worked very hard to get legislated. It fell under the provisions of criminal law and the state prosecutor pleaded the woman's case. I received a frantic call from my father that the police had arrested my brother and were taking him to jail. He was bailed out the following day. A friend of mine accompanied me to the jail gate to be met by my brother in a very buoyant mood because he had been befriended by the jail *dada* who had offered him protection in exchange for English lessons.

My brother and his wife had both been living at the edge of consciousness, alternating between drugs and alcohol. Physical abuse was a logical corollary to their drug-induced paranoia. To file a case against my brother was justifiable, albeit the abuse was mutual. However, to name my father and my dead mother as respondents was a scene from the theatre of the absurd and begged the existential question. The case was registered in Patiala Court and, thanks to these two irresponsible adults and my frequent visits to the court, I learnt to reverse park in the overcrowded parking lot.

They came as adversaries, saw each other, momentarily fell in love, and more often than not went off to a coffee house and failed to show up for the hearing, leaving my father and me to witness many others with similar complaints anxiously awaiting justice for hours on end. Eventually the magistrate, in extreme exasperation, dismissed the case and threw out the two truants with a stern warning to my sister-in-law not to waste the court's time.

We were confronted by the practice of 'co-wife' in states like Gujarat and Maharashtra. On the surface it appeared to be a social acknowledgement of the 'other woman', a romantic, noble gesture, but then consider the anguish of her lawful wife and the contractual wife? What about the cloak of shame children born out of marriage wore throughout their lives, slinking in the shadow of their legitimate siblings. The question that kept arising during all our meetings was whether any child was really illegitimate. It singed our sensibilities and obliged us to confront the duplicity that lay within state-sanctioned customary laws. To push the courts to acknowledge legitimacy and decree equal property rights for a child from such a union was a major victory for all the women's and a few civil liberties' groups that had joined hands in the initiative. It strengthened our belief that we still lived in a civilized country notwithstanding the many instances of state-sponsored oppression, or the countless massacres of poor Muslims and Harijans euphemistically termed 'riots'. That justice might be delayed but would eventually triumph. We never paused for a moment to either question ourselves or the constitutional authority: we were there to change the world.

The underlying principle of counselling and supporting individual women was that we all worked from the same feminist perspective. It was never 'we and them'. We were all bound together in the larger circle of sisterhood of gender biases, and oppression. I was then in the throes of an intense heartbreak. Another friend, a veteran of two divorces, was struggling to maintain her faith in relationships; a third struggling to emerge from the closet. It was a very bonding experience. They would say, '*Didi aap ka admi bhi aapko maarta hai*?', and when I spoke to them, they would say '*Aap to parhi likhi hain, itni strong ho, to aap ko kyon?*' I looked at their struggles to survive cruel, oppressive marriages and attempts to eke out a life of dignity. I was also very conscious that I did not want my daughter to emulate the model in which the basic principles of marriage were compromised. In my own life I had made the decision to leave the man I had married. I told myself, for me he is like a drug. I had to stop experiencing that 'rejected woman' syndrome. That feeling of constantly being pulled down in the face of everyone else's love and respect. On the one hand there was my family and my friends who made me feel really good about my life, on the other this man who belittled me and described me as a zero, making me genuinely believe that was all I really was.

During the first 10 years in Saheli we thought that the women who came to us would become stronger and form Saheli branches in their areas. Saheli would be a long chain of feminist perspectives on coping with life. That unfortunately did not happen and it was very frustrating. The most that those who came to us did when confronted with a problem, was that they would bring in others. We later realized that once these women received help, because they were the product of such a rigid lower or middle class morality, they didn't wish to talk about it to their neighbours and feel a sense of shame. There was therefore no prospect of Saheli developing a chain of branches as we had initially hoped. However, given the keen insights we received from the women with whom we had interacted in the complexities of tradition, caste, class, education, inherited property rights, maintenance, and their lack of self-confidence, we gained a clear understanding of the kinds of amendments necessary to the existing legislation that was failing to adequately protect women's rights.

•

Sometime in the late 1970s, a fragile diminutive woman called Bunny Page entered our chaotic lives of parenthood, work, 'must go' meetings, and late night parties. This, notwithstanding the necessity of waking up the following morning to face the pressures of another hectic day. Tackling daily the innumerable demands made on us (which continue to be made), we had evolved into multi-tasking superwomen with many more arms than goddess Durga herself. Bunny quietly but firmly introduced the idea of working with craftspeople and extricating them from the clutches of rapacious middlemen. This was a service which the Central Cottage Industries, the various state emporia, and the Khadi and

Village Industry Corporation were expected to provide but were doing very erratically and ineffectively. Bunny was a hybrid among us, with our casual ethnic attire. large powdered bindis, which so frequently streaked across our foreheads, *kajal* which often went feral and left us with racoon-like eyes, we revelled in our cheap handloom sarees and Kolhapuris, our seasonal ittars, and our cloth *jholas*. In contrast, there she was, an exceptionally well-dressed woman in her stilettos or boots, tapered skirts with a beautiful, casual ethnic scarf thrown across her shoulder, or sporting an amazing Bangladesh *kantha* blouse. Her accent was upper crust British, and she did not speak Hindi, although she had lived in Delhi through school and college. Her Parsi genes did not gel well with native languages; besides, she had married an Englishman working for the UN, they having met as amateur actors in Yatrik plays. Bunny also had a habit of referring to people as 'that what's your name' or that 'thingame'. No, she certainly was not 'our type'. However, our ridiculous inverted snobbery paled against Bunny's vision of offering an alternative to craftspeople, a vision she had carried over from Bangladesh. There she and a friend had been in the nascent stage of forming such an organization just when her husband was posted to India. They had been working on a scheme to directly expose the consumer to the people who made the beautiful crafts which adorned their homes and bodies. The idea was to boost sales of these by generating new designs and uses even while retaining and incorporating the traditional craft vocabulary. The dream she presented to us was to serve as a catalyst for the crafts sector, the second largest arena of the self-employment in India. The idea was to organize it into a federation so that craftspeoples' individual voices would be strong and heeded by governments, politicians, and the central Planning Commission. Crafts were not dying but the craftspeople had over the years being choked by the 'plastic' world viewed as progress.

Seven of us, founder members, overwhelmed by Bunny's insistence and commitment, came together to form Dastkar. The first Dastkar Bazar was held in the small park adjacent to the Defence Colony roundabout with 11 crafts-groups displaying their wares.

Dastkar opened up to me another aspect of Delhi that had existed for many centuries before we became a Republic. We went exploring the small bylanes of Old

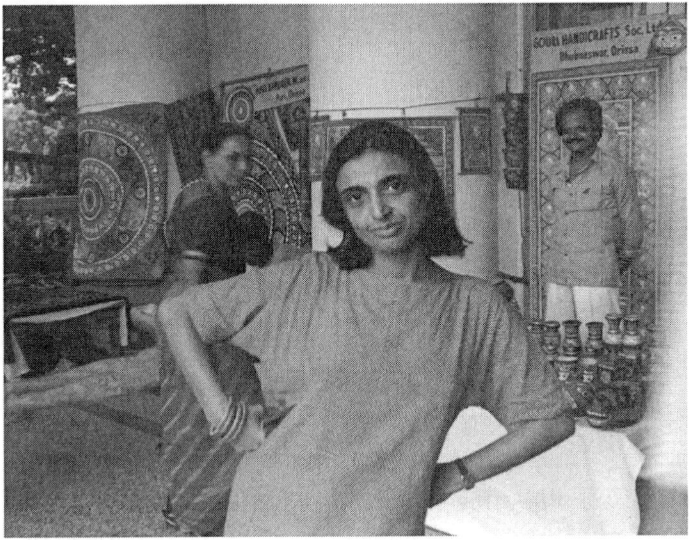

Bunny Page (Courtesy: Vipul Sangoi).

Delhi which stretched from Ajmeri Gate to Kashmiri Gate to meet artisans who were employed in creating exquisite hand-crafted objects, out of buffalo and other such large animal bones (as ivory was banned). There were the *zardozi karigars*, coppersmiths hand-beating large and small pots, some inscribed with Islamic calligraphy, others with delicately carved floral motifs, and leather binders of books. All the crafts and trades of their forefathers were still alive and flourishing, although they themselves, the creators, were not recipients of the respect or remuneration they deserved. Into that male bastion walked two alien women, Bunny and I, one with a limited common vocabulary, the other stumbling over her Urdu (the commonly spoken language in that area). After many weeks of such interaction we were eventually taken to one of the bone-carving *karkhana*s, to discover to our horror a Dickensian establishment. We were ushered into a large underground room lit by a few powerful naked bulbs, small slits for ventilation at the level of the ceiling, and rows of desks and chairs with naked wiring criss-crossing the tables. Sitting hunched over their respective tables were young boys, among whom the eldest could not have been over 15 years of age. They were breathing in the limited oxygen available and bringing to life exquisitely carved figurines. The tables were separated according to the task. While at one the raw material was sized and cut, at the other the outlines were carved. At the third the more delicate details of the figurine were carved, and the fourth polished it.

None of these boys was capable of producing the entire product. This was traditional craft at its wily worst. Little had changed for them since medieval times in the Delhi of the 1980s. There could never be a united demand for a better work environment and higher wages. Their vulnerability to the mastercraftsmen, some the recipients of the President's medal, was only too apparent. This was evidenced by the prominently displayed photograph of the master himself. Every celebrated craft worker in Delhi (or elsewhere) had the same story, be it the *zardozi* worker, the furniture wood-inlay worker, or the coppersmith (whose craft I fear will soon be lost forever).

The next couple of months we walked down those lanes interacting with potential partners, getting to know them better. They were invariably courteous, nodding their heads in agreement to all we said, and exploring whether we could help them avail of government aid. Then one day, after gaining several kilos of weight gorging ourselves on kababs and jalebis in Chandni Chowk's narrow gullies, we realized that we were being taken for a ride. They had no intention whatsoever of becoming Dastkar partners, because this would not suit any of the top operators, their *thekedar*s. The latter's proverb of 'maximum profit at minimum production cost', especially as their buyers, primarily exporters, believed that child labour was the easiest and most inexpensive path to the achievement of their goal.

Over the years, Dastkar has flourished and grown to where it is today through its members' close interaction with craftspersons in other parts of the country, but the craftspeople in Delhi have steered clear of it.

•

Our interaction at Saheli with a couple of prostitutes, their madam, and a 'social worker' from GB Road introduced me to another Delhi which had flourished pre-Independence with far greater grace and decorum than now. They wanted to form a union and asked us to help. We often visited them, but again were exposed to only what they wanted us to see. Exploitation by the police, lack of any government medical dispensaries, schools for the children born in GB Road, and the expression of prejudice and scorn of a largely hypocritical society within whose shadows they lived as outcasts. It was rumoured that the police paid bribes to their posting department to get transferred to Daryaganj police station which was amongst the most coveted posts for unaccounted earnings. I had visited the fringe of GB Road through my college days and later that delightful lane called Nai Sarak which is a treasure-house of old and second-hand books, but never thought of venturing into the adjacent gullies.

Working many years later on HIV/AIDS and combating once more layers of prejudice among educated professionals, when they cloaked their inner fears with counter-arguments on tradition and family values, I would exasperatedly counter their biases with 'Yes, 1.5 billion Indians were immaculately conceived.' A small group began working with eunuchs and young boys in their destined 'pick-up' places so that they could at least be informed about the threat of HIV and how they could protect themselves.

•

Delhi street theatre began to be closely associated with political theatre by the late 1970s and mid-'80s, and came of age with the emergence of Jana Natya Manch (popularly known as Janam, meaning 'birth' in Hindi). The members of Jana Natya Manch, with Safdar Hashmi, a member of the Communist Party of India (Marxist), as its informal spokesperson, was formed by a group of young men and women who were deeply committed to secularism and egalitarianism. These were principles that had been the hallmark of the generation of students and young adults who had opted to join M.K. Gandhi's call to join the national struggle for Independence. This spirit and urge to rewrite our history was what motivated hundreds of young people to leave comfortable and secure jobs to find their true calling in working towards greater equality among the people of India. They were attempting to bridge the vast chasm between the top 10 per cent of privileged Indians and the 0 per cent whose voice rarely reached the corridors of power. Janam's plays highlighted the total lack of all amenities/rights that had been promised by the Constitution to every citizen of India. The scripts of the plays were developed bearing in mind the ground realities of the oppression of common people. They ranged from sketches about the lives of farm labour and factory workers, to themes of communal tension. All focused people's attention on the divisive manipulation of politicians across party lines. The plays were performed at the most inhospitable locales, deriving intense satisfaction from success in igniting a defiant spark among the underprivileged. All the scripts of the plays, songs, and poetry were developed within the group, with Safdar Hashmi leading the discussions on pluralism, class oppression, and the roots of poverty. The group lived under the weight of the hostility of the state machinery, landlords, politicians, and industrialists, who viewed them as potential instigators of civil and labour agitation and unrest. On 1 January 1989, Safdar Hashmi and Janam were brutally attacked while performing a street play in solidarity with the striking factory workers of Sahibabad (a rapidly growing industrial belt on the outskirts of Delhi) entitled *Halla Bol* (Raise Your Voice). The following day, at the age of 34 he died of his injuries.

His death generated a wave of grief and shock, immediately touching all Dilliwallahs irrespective of their political affiliations. Even that large apolitical section of people who rarely involved themselves with public issues were moved and mourned his loss. It aroused too a nationwide wave of outrage as Indians came together on that one occasion to express grief and solidarity. He was not a Naxalite but a social activist, and the shock-waves of his death shook the youth and millions of Indians throughout India who believe that

dissent is a basic prerequisite for an evolving democracy. The brutal violence unleashed that day on a group of activists was to have far-reaching consequences and his murder was always remembered as an example of the state's connivance in muzzling the voices of dissent for petty political ends. On this occasion the violence had been instigated by Mukesh Sharma, a member of the Congress party, a municipal council aspirant who feared losing the election to Ramanand of the CPM.

Safdar Hashmi's funeral procession on 3 January 1989 was among the largest voluntary gathering of people in Delhi. The following day, Janam, with Moloyashree Hashmi (Safdar's wife), returned to Jhandapur to resume the interrupted play.

Sahmat was formed in the aftermath of Safdar's death and it was decided that this group would be an artist-run collective and not be affiliated to the CPM. Today it has become one of the largest social activist groups who carry their core message of 'Unity in Diversity' in the form of an annual roaming art exhibition, taking the cue from Art as activism in India fostered by P.C. Joshi, general secretary of the CPI in the 1940s.

Mourners bidding farewell to Safdar Hashmi, Delhi, 1989 (Courtesy: The Sahmat Collective).

- 14 -

Janata Party, Pant Nagar, Billa-Ranga, Suresh Ram

In June 1978 the Janata government's continuing row over leadership of the party, with a plethora of aspirants to prime-ministership, led the home minister Chaudhary Charan Singh, under whose party banner and symbol the elections had been fought, to pull out of the government. It was becoming clear to many of us that the people's heroes who had been jailed throughout the the Emergency who had come together under a single banner to fight the general election to defeat Indira and Sanjay Gandhi, their coterie, and the Congress party, had feet of clay. They were merely motivated by private ambitions rather than the public good, and had little faith in one another. A plethora of personal ambitions continued to surface; perceived and genuine grievances began fracturing the unity of the Janata Party. We lost faith in our 'war heroes' almost a month into their oath of allegiance to the people of India.

The atrocities of the Provisional Armed Constabulary (PAC), who had opened fire killing over 200 (although the official figure given was 13) daily wage farm labourers, ruthlessly suppressing their strike against the administration of the Pant Nagar Agriculture and Research University had shaken us to the core. A colleague from the PUCL (as it happened, also a PhD student at JNU) and I reached Pant Nagar two days after the brutal murders on a fact finding mission. We discovered that all that the labour was demanding was permanency of employment as the university had violated all labour laws by hiring daily wage workers on a monthly basis rather than laying them off for five days a month as stipulated by law. The administration had in this way been flouting the law, a serious misdemeanour, for over a decade.

We were shocked at the callous attitude of the 'new' government and even of a majority of journalists. The latter were too preoccupied either positioning and ingratiating themselves with the new dispensation as the media élite, or just so relieved that they could reinvent themselves as protagonists of an 'invisible' anti-Emergency movement. No one was inclined to listen to us. The Emergency had been lifted and the Fourth Estate had more serious issues to report. Our investigation of what actually happened in the university was of no significance to most as the passionate honeymoon between the newly elected government and the media was still ongoing. We were eventually advised by an older champion of our cause that we needed to expand our group and align ourselves with a few senior journalists who had the ear of the government and the press. We were introduced to our heroes of the independent press who patiently heard us through, but most were too busy fine-tuning the manifesto of the Janata Party to pay attention to the firing on and consequent deaths of labourers. They suggested however that the organization should adopt a broader focus than 'Justice for Pant Nagar', which led to the formation of 'Justice for Democracy' as a body to combat and thwart any possibility of a recurrence of the Emergency.

We limped back into our lives feeling very guilty

at having let down the labourers who had placed their trust in us. The compensation was a joke, the leaders, or rather those who lived to tell their tale, were sacked, and the commission of enquiry made life monetarily easier for the few retired officials who constituted it. It died its natural death, as have many such commissions before and after, with little or no relief to the victims. The PAC continued to wreak havoc on the lives of the disenfranchised of this country.

•

Into this very bleak scenario, the events of 26 and 28 August 1978 rocked Delhi into a state of shock. Geeta and Sanjay Chopra were children of a captain in the Indian Navy. They lived in the Armed Services Colony in Dhaula Kuan and had left their home at 6 p.m. to participate in a *Yuva Vani* panel of All India Radio. They were bright, attractive children. Geeta, 17 years old, was a second year student at Jesus and Mary College and her 14 year old brother a student of Modern School. *Yuva Vani* was a very popular youth programme and it was a great honour to be selected for one of their talk-shows.

The siblings hitched a lift till Gole Dak Khana, a common practice which made life easier for many young people, as the buses were invariably late, erratic, and overcrowded. Auto–rickshaws, as is their practice to this day, were moody, whimsical, and overcharged. The youngsters were scheduled to reach All India Radio at 7 p.m. and their father was to collect them at 9 p.m.

They never made it to the *Yuva Vani* panel, having been kidnapped en route by Kuljeet Singh (alias Ranga Khus) and Jasbir Singh (alias Billa), habitual criminals who had recently come to Delhi to evade the Bombay police. Their plan was to kidnap the siblings and demand a ransom as the two were well-dressed, spoke English, and appeared to be from a wealthy family. Their plans soon misfired when a couple of travellers on the same route saw a girl pulling the driver's hair, screaming for help, and a boy grappling with a man sitting on the passenger seat. Citizens of Delhi in those days had a keener sensitivity to the distress of others in public places than they do today. The good samaritans tried to stop the car and a couple of them noted its number. One of them rang up the police control room to give details of what he had witnessed. The operator incorrectly recorded the number. Another reported it to the Rajinder Nagar police station, where the man in charge claimed it was a cognizable offence and beyond the jurisdiction of their office. The frantic parents, after spending many hours looking for their children, filed a police complaint. So much wasted time by those who should have moved swiftly and thwarted the crime.

The bodies of the siblings were found on 28 August by a cowherd grazing his herd on the ridge near Buddha Jayanti Park. Witnesses corroborated that they had seen the two men, the siblings, and the car there on the 26th evening. Both the bodies bore marks of multiple stab wounds, had broken collar bones, and deep lacerations. The bodies were so decomposed that it was difficult to ascertain whether Geeta had been raped. She had in fact been raped by both, a confession made by the criminals in police custody. The father went to the press and Delhi woke up from its self-imposed stupor as it witnessed the shenanigans of the Janata Party. These were not poor slum-dwellers' children but the children of a senior captain in the Indian Navy. If it could happen to them, then who was safe in the city? The crime aroused a deep sense of apprehension amongst middle- and upper middle-class families. The government swung into action, the culprits were apprehended on 8 September 1978 on a train travelling to Bombay. Again, the apprehension was not the work of the police but of jawans of the Indian army when Billa and Ranga had jumped into a carriage reserved for them. The culprits were tried in both the High Court and the Supreme Court, the latter upholding the death penalty. They received no clemency from the President of India and were executed in 1982. Both the siblings were awarded the Kirti Chakra on 5 April 1981 and the Council for Child Welfare instituted two annual bravery awards for children under 16 in the names of Geeta Chopra and Sanjay Chopra.

The case set a precedent, henceforth permitting journalists to interview prisoners on death row. Prabha Dutt, a journalist, had petitioned the court when refused permission to do so by the jail authorities. The Supreme Court granted the right to interviews, provided the prisoner was agreeable.

In July 1978 Morarji Desai was obliged to accept Charan Singh back into his cabinet as finance minister. In November Indira Gandhi returned to parliament, having won the by-election in Chikmangalur in Karnataka. In

July 1979 the Janata Party finally fell and Charan Singh became the caretaker prime minister.

•

An amusing sidelight to the Janata Party government and illustrative of the confusion that reigned was the Suresh Ram incident. Two 'foot-soldiers' from the JP Narayan movement discovered that Jagjivan Ram's son, Suresh Ram, had been using a friendly member of parliament's room in Western Court as a rendevous for his sexual escapades. One of them, with a fine nose for ferretting out scandals went there and confronted Suresh Ram and his lady friend. They bundled the couple into Suresh's Mercedes Benz and had them driven to Ghaziabad. Never having travelled in a Merc before, our 'moral policeman' fiddling curiously with all the nobs on the dashboard, inadvertently opened the glove compartment. Out popped over a dozen photographs of Suresh Ram in poses out of the *Kama Sutra*. They disregarded Suresh Ram's plea that the photographs if made public would jettison his father, Jagjivan Ram's, prospects of becoming prime minister and spurned offers of bribes in return for the photographs. The photographs were first shown to Charan Singh who blinked and could barely believe his eyes. Another leader of the coalition party examined them very carefully and said he could not endorse the publication of such photos (honour among thieves). They were then taken to Indira Gandhi (we were told by Khushwant Singh) who looked at them with a keen eye which was neither prudish nor shocked and passed them on to her daughter-in-law Maneka, the editor of *Surya* magazine. That edition of *Surya* was completely sold out within an hour of hitting the stands. All hell broke loose. Incidentally, the hero of the 'sting operation' is now himself the proud owner of his own Mercedes.

•

Weary of the Janata's Party's continuing political infighting, inefficiency, and shananigans, the people of India once again put their faith in the Congress, or more explicitly in Indira Gandhi in the general elections of January 1980. The elections were masterminded by her son Sanjay Gandhi, who also selected most of the candidates. Many from his coterie were elected as first time members of parliament. The old practice within the Congress party of democratically electing candidates had been gradually bypassed by Indira Gandhi, and the 1980 elections set another benchmark for the rise of the Gandhis' authoritarian manner of functioning. It was apparent to most of us that Indira Gandhi seemed irretrievably under the influence of her son Sanjay.

Fate however intervened and Sanjay Gandhi died in a plane accident in June 1980. It was a stunning turn of events, and the majority of Indians, notwithstanding their very superstitious sensibilities on matters of death, heaved a collective sigh of relief.

Rajiv Gandhi was persuaded to enter politics.

- 15 -

The Asian Games and the Changing Face of Delhi

Prior to the Asian Games, New Delhi had been a low-rise city. The only skyscrapers, a word now used for multistorey buildings, were in the area around Connaught Place, Nehru Place, and Bhikaiji Cama Place. The city was largely a sprawl of single- and double-storey residential colonies built to accommodate the refugee families that had fled to Delhi at Partition, and the verdant expanse of Lutyens's original New Delhi, where lived senior government officials, politicians, and the affluent of the colonial era. Five-star hotels could be counted and named without much thought. Only a smattering of flyovers existed and traffic intersections were just a comma in an intra-city journey. Roads on most stretches were two-laned and sufficiently wide to accommodate buses and trucks, Ambassadors and Fiats, two- and three-wheelers plying at moderate speeds. Pollution was not a common word. As far as sporting arenas go, the National Stadium, the aging workhorse of the 1951 inaugural Asian Games, and Feroz Shah Kotla, the grand old cricket ground, were the only ones of any stature.

Pragati Maidan was the first large-scale public development enterprise prior to the Asian games. It became part of our entertainment circuit in the early 1970s, after the inauguration of the first international trade fair which was held to celebrate 25 years of India's independence. Incidentally, the trade fair triggered the first traffic jams in the city (leaving us Dilliwallahs more bemused than frustrated). The vast open space of the Maidan held many attractions. Although really crackling to life during winter when numerous fairs were held, it was nevertheless a venue where one could meet incognito all year round. It had a cinema hall, Shakuntalam, seating only 300, but where one could see movies, both Hindi and English, at the cheapest rates in town. The three gigantic permanent structures—or Halls as they are called—hit you in the face with their brutal modernity, making architecture an easy part of our vocabulary.

Each year a book fair would be held, where one was sure to find a title or two at a super discount. A few of us even got temporary jobs at some of the state pavilions giving us much needed pin money for a brief spell. As B was in the publishing world and had many friends and colleagues, our house became an after-working-hours 'salon' in which to unwind and have a good time. After a couple of days of entertaining all these British publishers I realised that the faces of even a 'white man' soon blur into 'much of the sameness'. I would be constantly addressing one for the other. So it is not as the British made us believe that oriental features are difficult to identify as individual faces — it happens to them as well.

The Trade Fair Authority of India has burgeoned into a mammoth programme for trade exhibitions throughout the year, bringing in big bucks for corporations and the government. Indeed, to such a degree that every space on Pragati Maidan's vast acres is now viewed through the lens of 'making financial sense'. As I write this, the shocking news is that the three Halls are going to be demolished by the government to make way for more

Within the Hall of Nations (Courtesy: Raj Rewal).

‘lucrative’ buildings. Hailed all over the world as works of architectural ingenuity and as marvels of engineering, the Hall of Nations complex and the Nehru Pavilion are

icons of our built heritage. They occupy less than two per cent of Pragati Maidan but sadly even these are to be sacrificed on the altar of Mammon.

The announcement that India had won her bid to host the 1982 Asian Games was made in 1976. It came at a time when the country was passing through its darkest

political phase. Indira Gandhi had declared a state of national emergency in June 1975 as a desperate measure to retain power in the face of an adverse court order and widespread opposition across India. In 1977, when general elections were finally held, Indira's Congress party was defeated by the newly-formed Janata Party. For the first time since 1947 a non-Congress government was in power at the Centre.

Inevitably, during those tumultuous years, India's commitment to host Asia's biggest sporting event had receded in public and government consciousness. Yet, in 1977, with the return of democratic normalcy, there were still five years to go; sufficient time to plan and organize a successful event. However, the lacklustre, divided, and squabbling Janata dispensation had little inclination to move the pieces forward. Its conservative leadership believed that the expenditure necessary to host the continent's gala sports meet to be frivolous and unnecessary. It took all of the Indian Olympic Association's vice-president, Vijay Kumar Malhotra's, energetic efforts to keep the prospects of the Games alive, albeit barely.

In 1980, with the Games just two years away, and now

Facing of the Hall of Nations (Courtesy: Raj Rewal).

in need of critical attention if they were to take place at all, the wobbly Janata coalition disintegrated. The dying flame of India's tenuous Asian Games affair suddenly flickered back to life. Indira and the Congress were back in power, and for several reasons, not least among them, a burning desire to restore her personal prestige, Indira Gandhi not only decided that the big event must be held, but it had better prove to be a resounding success.

The Asian Games of 1982 were whipped into national awareness. Forces and resources were mobilized. The old organizing committee of the Janata days was moribund and therefore a new one, bristling with well over 50 powerful government functionaries, was constituted. Plans for infrastructure were speeded up. Tussles for venues were resolved. The claim of the nondescript town of Rai in Haryana, which was being vigorously promoted by a regional Congress satrap, was rejected and Delhi given an emphatic and unequivocal mandate as the host city.

Indira assigned three commanders to win the two-year war against time and deliver the Asian Games to the nation. They were Buta Singh, Jagmohan, and her son, Rajiv. For Buta, helming the Games' organizing committee over these two years were to be his path to prominence and political reckoning. Jagmohan, as Delhi's Lieutenant Governor, kept the administration focused and on its toes. He emerged with a reputation of a man who was capable of taking on the ills of Delhi head on. For Rajiv, the reluctant freshman politician, it was true blooding: the first major assignment under his mother's protective watch. Through the two-year run up to the Games, all three were hands-on, and whatever the controversies and criticisms that grew around them, they certainly couldn't be faulted for taking their foot off the gas.

For two years the city was put through the wringer. It would be roughed, buffed, and equipped with an entirely new set of features that would, at any rate, ramp up its confidence and substance. These developments served as the springboard for the turbocharged phases of development that were to follow in the decades ahead.

Tenders were floated, designs approved, contracts awarded, and moneys sanctioned. Heavy construction machinery burst into action and tore into the somnolent terrain. The word went out and unskilled labour streamed into the capital, and this would subsequently prove to be one of the Achillies' heels of the Games as many of them never left, were never permanently settled, and continued to live in slums. Cranes and excavators worked through the night. The dust of construction hung heavy in the air and the city had its first prolonged experience of traffic snarls. By now, however, the Games had acquired celebrity status and these issues were not overly bemoaned. It was all part of the build-up to something momentous. One could sense a sneaking pride in what people saw as a kind of evolution of their city into a world-class capital.

Somewhere along the way, Appu was introduced. A caricature mascot of the Games, Appu was a hit. The rotund prancing elephant was given his own song, and together, in the months that preceded the games, jumbo and the jingle built up the mood. Quite rapidly, as huge structures of steel and concrete rose on the relatively level land, Delhi's low urban airspace began to acquire new dimensions. If there was one term that captured public imagination more than any other, it was 'flyover'. Somehow, these sleek arcs of unfettered tarmac were viewed as the epitome of modernity. They represented the cityscapes of developed countries, and their existence brought us on par with them. Delhi got seven flyovers as part of the Asian Games package. Some were illuminated by high-mast sodium bulbs. I remember wondering how they could raise such high poles and fit lights on top of them. For many months, driving across these spanking new flyovers was a memorable experience.

Jawaharlal Nehru Stadium was, of course, the most remarkable disrupter of the skyline. It grew out of a level wasteland between the Defence Colony and the new Sewa Nagar flyovers. Located as it was along arterial axes from central to south Delhi, JNS's development from embryonic beginnings to becoming a fully-fledged stadium was observed by commuters on an almost daily basis. With its criss-crossing members and massive circular shape it was *the* new view in town. From the flyovers, one's sight would be drawn to its dynamic shape, and if on the driver's seat, your eyes alternated between its considerable mass and the road ahead. At night, when the floodlights were switched on, the glow spread to a vast distance, high into the night sky.

The other huge stadium was Indraprastha, later renamed Indira Gandhi Indoor Stadium, an appropriation of the two signature architectural creations of the

Games for the Nehru-Gandhi big-building label. This giant was in the proximity of another busy area, just off where Ring Road bypassed the ITO (Income Tax Office) intersection. It even had a roof, and remarkably it was retractable. There was more than a one roof story around in those days. The hi-tech Talkatora swimming complex didn't get its much vaunted roof because it fell a victim to design controversies and thus never quite achieved the star status of its contemporaries. Then, on 19 November, the day of the Games' opening ceremony, coincidentally also Indira Gandhi's birthday, the ceiling of the weightlifting hall leaked amidst a heavy downpour. Soon the venue was flooded with the first event scheduled just hours later. Panic-stricken, the staff turned to Rajiv. He, in the never-say-die spirit of the ninth Asian Games endeavour, took personal charge, missed mummy's birthday celebrations, and camped through the night at site to supervise the repair and mopping operation. All was spick and span the following day before the first barbell rose.

The weightlifting arena stood in the Asiad Village. Architect Raj Rewal's high-density 'cluster-style' apartment complex built to host the thousands of visiting athletes and officials was a new concept in Delhi. Its landmark was the bulbous tower restaurant, which was supposed to be the Village's culinary destination. The Village site wiped out a designated green area adjoining the fourteenth-century ruins of Sultan Allauddin Khilji's city. It was an example of how Delhi's urban Master-plan was on occasion disregarded to accommodate the Games' infrastructure. This was because what should have been thoughtfully worked out and executed over half a dozen years had to be undertaken in an unavoidable, insensitive scramble in one-third that time. This was characteristic of India.

After the Games, the flats were allocated to government officials. The Village's premium aura was a factor in egging south Delhi's hitherto placid colonies to begin reconsidering and reinventing themselves, thereby kicking off what would snowball into a amazing and unseemly real estate boom over the next three decades.

Apart from athletes and officials, a huge influx of tourists and other visitors was anticipated during the Games' weeks and the existing hotels were not going to be able to cope. The private hospitality industry sensed a great opportunity and eagerly invested. A spate of five-

The Asian Games Residential Complex (Courtesy: Raj Rewal).

star hotel buildings began cropping up in addition to the other construction in progress. Some were government-owned and others were built by large international hotel chains. The city's skyline began acquiring another facet: a fashionable, luxurious slant, distinct from the regular construction of the time. This however was one story without a happy ending. Many of the hotels failed to

beat the clock. Come zero hour, they were struggling to ready their grand facilities. They needn't have been overly concerned because the expected influx never materialized. Hoteliers complained that the government had misled them by grossly exaggerating the expected numbers, and government officials countered that the hotels had in any case failed to meet the deadline. It was anticlimactic. Room occupancies were low and the hotel industry limped gloomily through the games to fight on another day.

As a sporting event, the Asian Games were a success. Over a million people came to the various sports venues every day. India placed fifth in the medals tally, behind China, Japan, and the two Koreas. (There was of course the shameful loss to Pakistan in the hockey final and that sparked its own murky stories.) Despite the rough edges, the sports infrastructure had served its purpose well and justified the sweat and finances that went into its creation. As a city, Delhi had proved itself. Exuberant talk was in the air of an Afro-Asian Games and, in the not too distant future, the Olympics. That was not to be. The city's next sporting event close to the scale of the Asian Games would come 28 years later. Sadly, lessons would not have been learnt, and once more, Delhi would be racing against time to put up a good show. On this occasion, however, there would be many red faces and much embarrassment.

One of the legacies of the Games was the changed skyline of the capital city; a skyline that would take on a life of its own and become uglier in the years that followed with too much more of the same. The features that were novel in 1982 slowly became the normal and even mundane. In the 1980s, ice-cream carts parked themselves strategically on the slopes of flyovers inviting people to halt and enjoy the 'heights'. Gradually however Ring Road was transformed into a chain of smog-ridden flyovers where stopping would result in a traffic tailback. Luxury hotels, in whose opulent lobbies one would feel self-conscious, lost their mystique. Apathy crept back and engulfed the sports establishment, and the stadia, even while in use, slid into disrepair. Even so, many of these edifices and constructions continued to endure as reference points. The Games did their bit for the city, but sadly the city thereafter did too much to itself.

•

Television came of age at around the same time as the Asian Games, with the primary objective of livetelecasting programmes to as wide a viewership as it was possible to reach. From the early experiments, to extending the services to seven more cities by 1975, we were suddenly overwhelmed by colour television, multiple choice of television sets although no imports were permitted, and soft loans extended by nationalized banks for the purchase of TV sets. The strident criticism of the costs arising from mismanagement and delay in the construction of much of the planned infrastructure, and the consequent extreme inconvenience to the people of Delhi, all came to a halt as Dilliwallahs sat glued to the small screen. Not even the unsuccessful performance of most of our sportsmen and women could dampen their enthusiasm.

Calcutta had the distinction of introducing colour television coverage in February 1982 during the first Nehru Hockey Cup tournament which was held in Eden Gardens. India's small-screen programming began in the early 1980s with two blockbuster tele-serials of the epics *Ramayana* and *Mahabharata*, which notched up world record viewership for a single programme. India stood still every Sunday glued to TV sets, lapping up a very regressive interpretation of the two epics. These reinforced the most myopic perceptions of Hindu 'traditions', reinterpreting the definition of nationalism to a level of jingoism. The early seeds of post-Partition communalism were, I believe, sown in the comfort of people's drawing rooms and are reflected in what we are witnessing today.

However, on a more positive note, as more people began owning TV sets, Doordarshan opened up several new channels. Also, simultaneously, and indeed a little prior to the airing of the epics, the flowering of Doordarshan's creativity reached a peak with shows like *Hum Log* (1984), *Wagle ki Duniya* (1988), *Buniyaad* (1986-87), and comedy shows like *Yeh Jo Hai Zindagi*,and later *Bharat Ek Khoj*, *The Sword of Tipu Sultan*, and *Chandrakanta*. Hindi film song-based programmes like *Chitrahaar*, *Rangoli*, *Superhit Muqabla,* and crime-thrillers like *Karamchand*, *Byomkesh Bakshi*, and *Malgudi Days* followed. Some of these were extremely popular with children. As I did not own a TV set, Nikhat was deprived of some of these, particularly *Malgudi Days,* and had to rest content with my reading out the stories to her.

In 1991, faced by an acute foreign exchange crisis, P.V. Narasimha Rao initiated a series of economic reforms, including the liberalization of the broadcasting industry, opening it up to cable television. This led to an explosion in the Indian cable TV industry. Rupert Murdoch was a favoured foreign beneficiary. Star TV eclipsed all other networks, although a multitude of Hindi and regional language channels were introduced with a plethora of news channels. The rest is history. I finally bought our first TV set which was housed in a cabinet to be rolled out on its wheels for specific programmes only.

- 16 -

Delhi in Flames

31 October 1984 was just another day at Saheli. A young woman with two very young children had walked in seeking shelter because her husband had summarily ejected her from their home. I rang Nizamuddin Police Station with whom, over the years, we had forged a good working relationship. The Station House Officer came on the line to inform us, strain and tension clouding his sentences, that no work could be accomplished that day as Indira Gandhi had just been shot by one of her bodyguards and was being rushed to the All India Medical Institute. The time was 11.45 a.m. and the news was blurted out spontaneously by a saddened and stunned SHO much before the official announcement was made. I immediately rang some of my friends in the

media, but none of them had a clear indication of what had happened. One said he had heard that she had been shot, but was it fatal?

We stayed glued to our radio through the day but, apart from the SHO's shocked indiscretion, no further information was forthcoming. Rumour fed off speculation and fear. All we did learn was that the two bodyguards were Sikhs. I immediately recalled my mother narrating to us the shock, immense pain, and a sense of disbelief when another assassination had taken place on the morning of 30 January 1948. She told us that for those few minutes, which had seemed like a lifetime, all of them had virtually stopped breathing. They had feared that the assassin might be a Muslim or a Sikh, and anticipated another bloodbath so close to the carnage of August 1947. She would be in tears when she confessed that although the pain of losing the father of the nation was immense, it became tinged with a sense of relief when Nathuram Godse's name was announced as the assassin. Thankfully, there would be no aftermath of bloodshed and carnage. How could I forget this story, narrated by one (my mother) who was from a minority religion, never secure in the protection of the big brother?

Salma Sultan, a Doordarshan newsreader, was the first to announce Indira Gandhi's death in the evening.

By evening, when I left Saheli to go home, the crowd around the All India Institute of Medical Sciences (AIIMS) had multiplied to many thousands and I could hear slogans inflamed by hatred seeking the heads of the perpetrators. It took less than 30 minutes for me to reach home, and by then the radio and TV news had announced her death, with slightly garbled news of Sikhs being targeted — one had indeed been burnt to death near the AIIMS. Even the President of India's, Zail Singh's, motorcade bringing him to Rashtrapati Bhawan from an international tour, was pelted with stones.

My Sikh father-in-law was awaiting me, tense at what might happen. He who had witnessed the worst Partition riots in Calcutta and had lost his father in Montgomery district while pruning his roses to a Muslim overcome by hatred who had recently arrived from Delhi. My father-in-law was well aware of the enormous violence that an armed crowd inflamed by a deep sense of grievance and bias was capable of. The sheer madness of a mob, inflamed, baying for blood, secure that no force could stop them from achieving their objectives. They had power in numbers, armed with weapons, and the confidence that the state police forces could not or would not act against them.

The father of my four year old daughter had just left us a fortnight prior to this to live with his girlfriend. My mother-in-law, an Assamese, was with her relatives in Calcutta. On the one hand, we, my daughter and I, were not coping very well with the pain and loss of all that we had believed would be permanent. On the other, there was my father-in-law's extreme vulnerability and fear conditioned by the post-Partition massacres. These I, who had been born post-Independence, had not witnessed and could not experience with the same intensity and foreboding as him: the fury of a maddened mob. Yes, I had been deeply shaken by the massacres in Nellie but from a distance. Not being a witness to mass murders or even a single murder, distances one from the extremities of pain, fear, and recurrent nightmares that can haunt one forever. The news reports gave a lie to my notional sense of safety. By late that night we could hear the drum-beats of the mobs in not very distant Munirka. Fires seemed to be scarring the night sky with a menacing crimson. Our prime minister had been assassinated and my father-in-law wondered aloud how many more would be sacrificed on the altar of revenge. We felt emotionally unprotected and vulnerable, he most of all as he wore a turban.

By midday on 1 November all news coverage was focused on the assassination of Indira Gandhi, with quotations from dignitaries from around the world, couched in the usual banalities of official bereavement messages. The radio and TV continually played funereal music and all that was showing on TV was the coverage of dignitaries walking in and out of 1A Safdarjung Road, Indira Gandhi's residence.

A few of my friends called me to join them on a silent march through the lanes of Munirka where it was rumoured that knives and swords were being sharpened through the night and kerosene collected in huge jerrycans. I could not have left my little daughter and father-in-law. The latter had informed me that if the mob came, and they would because they had begun stalking the Vasant Vihar gurudwara, he would hide in the water tanks breathing air through an ineffectual straw. He advised me to take my daughter and stay with close Hindu friends of mine a block away. This was indeed the advice proffered by many senior bureaucrats and politicians, including the Sikh president of India, to whoever among the Sikhs requested help and protection. My friend came and collected my daughter and her ayah, but I could not leave Baba alone. This was particularly so because we had no clear idea in which direction our servants would sway if questioned. Fortunately, B drove into the house just as the mob had begun gathering outside the gate. As he does not wear a turban he was able to walk out of his car and convince them that no Sardar lived there; that there once had been some, but they had since left.

In the midst of this very tense environment I received a call from my mother to say that my father had decided to don a saffron turban, taken out his shotgun, and handed a rifle to my younger brother. That he was threatening to walk out into the mob in Munirka loudly proclaiming: '*Jo bole so nihal, Sat Sri Akal*', the war-cry of Guru Gobind Singh, the last of the ten Sikh gurus. It would have been bizarrely comic had this occurred at another time, another place, but this mob meant business. She had told him in no uncertain terms that he should abandon his histrionics and bravado as he had not witnessed the carnage of Partition when he had been safely cocooned at his university campus in the US.

By the morning of 2 November I had joined my friends, *sahelis*, and civil liberty groups in a desperate bid to gather as much relief as possible for the poor women and children of Trilokpuri, perhaps the worst scene of atrocities and bloodshed in the entire city of Delhi. Here, by then, a few of the men who had survived, were bolted into their homes or had taken refuge with a few kindly Hindu neighbours, unaware of the multitudinous bodies, mutilated, charred, stabbed, or hacked to death, strewn in the narrow gullies. None had been spared, not husbands, fathers, brothers, or sons.

Food, water, medical assistance ... innumerable hurried lists were prepared and volunteers set off to gather whatever they could. A friend and I decided on 3 November that we should go and ask hotels for surplus food and request the management to package it and water. As we knew the management of the Taj Hotel on Mansingh Road, that was our first port of call. There we encountered some film stars and directors, some of whom we knew, while they awaited their limousines. They were all attired for Indira Gandhi's cremation in what were later referred to as page 3 funeral garments, and completely oblivious of what else was happening in Delhi. Ignorant or just plain disinterested, notwithstanding the fact that some newspapers had carried front-page news reporting the death of over 3,000 Sikhs, and counting. I met one of them many years later, an actor famous for his 'camera memory'. He immediately recognized me as 'that militant he had seen on the staircase of the Taj Hotel'. The management informed us that they were (under the Food and Beverages regulation) not permitted to distribute surplus food; not even in emergency situations and had to regularly consign it to the garbage. The Manager handed us Rs 1,000 as his personal contribution. The general consensus was that the Sikhs had really got out of hand and had it coming to them. This was a sentiment I was to hear repeatedly expressed over the following fortnight. It was echoed too by the kind, upper crust volunteers sorting out clothes and food in Lajpat Bhawan hall which had been requisitioned for this purpose by the newly formed Nagrik Ekta Manch. Surprisingly, it was the first sentence uttered by my mother-in-law after greeting me when she returned to Delhi, just a week after her husband had planned to jump into a water tank, as did the husband of another Sikh friend.

Throughout the following three days the city was gripped by fear until the evening of 4 November when the army and paramilitary forces were belatedly ordered to control the mobs who were being encouraged and supported by sycophants of the Congress party (as has subsequently been revealed through survivor narratives). The names of the same well-known Congress leaders repeatedly surfaced in different accounts: these were leaders who believed that no law would or could convict them and the conclusions voiced by subsequent commissions have sadly proved this to be true. Virtually all the leaders cited continue to wield influence in the public sphere.

The horrific events of 1984 recalled for some of us stories of the historical ethnic purges of the Holocaust and, closer to home, the many bloody massacres of Muslims, euphemistically termed 'communal riots' in independent India. The first camp was organized for the homeless traumatized survivors in the staff quarters of the newly constructed Farash Bazar police station. They came clinging to one another, the elders recalling their harrowing experiences during Partition. Each horrifying day rolled into the next, with another chapter of grim

Passages from the aftermath, Delhi, 1984 (Courtesy: Ram Rahman).

accounts of human depravity. On 2 November a friend, who thought she knew the Gandhi household really well, persuaded me and another colleague to accompany her to 1 Safdarjung Road and appeal directly to Rajiv Gandhi. We were not permitted to enter, which was understandable given the tight ring of security that surrounded them. The plan was to reach someone close to him who could apprise him of the dire predicament of thousands of innocent people, many of whom had overnight become widows and orphans, mothers whose sons were dead, or a combination of these. We were able to persuade his cousin, the very individual who subsequently advised Rajiv to open the locks of Babri Masjid, to come to the gate. His distraction was palpable and we were informed that nothing could be done until the cremation. All available security personnel had been deployed for the single purpose of ensuring that the cremation of our late prime minister should go off without a hitch, so another day of carnage with impunity ensued.

Although the army had been deployed on 3 November, they awaited helplessly and expectantly on the sidelines as violence raged around them because the Commissioner of Police had withheld the order authorizing them to act. It was only on the fourth day after Rajiv Gandhi had toured the areas struck with death and destruction that the police extended full cooperation to the army and worked in tandem to quell the violence. In the camps, a day after law and order was enforced by the army, an uneasy silence pervaded, almost as if in breathless anticipation of some good news. We witnessed tears of joy, punctuated simultaneously by the high-pitched wails of those who had lost hope. Not one mother, wife, or child could wholeheartedly celebrate the cessation of four bloody days as they grieved in solidarity with those left with no hope. We spent the entire day in camp, ineffectually attempting to offer whatever support we could. In the midst of this misery we were informed that H.K.L. Bhagat, one of the names we had been hearing as a key Congressman who had supported the mobs, was planning to visit the camp. The news was brought by his emissary, along with truckloads of food and medicine. For the first time the collective pain, especially of the women, turned to anger and they had the trucks sent away. We could scarcely believe that such act of crass arrogance and insensitivity could become a reality and had forgotten how thick-skinned politicians can be and are. Equally revolting were the actions of the survivors from the merchant class, the self-proclaimed male Sikh leaders of the camp, with vested interests. They ingratiatingly accepted the token 'aid', turning a blind eye to the atrocities that had occurred. H.K.L. Bhagat and his cohorts slunk into the camp at around 8 p.m. and sneaked up to the office of the District Police Commissioner on an invitation, we later learnt, from the mercenary merchants themselves. Word reached the grieving widows who gathered at the foyer, weeping and totally overcome by grief.

I rushed there in a rage to be astonished at the sight of H.K.L. Bhagat sitting behind the DCP's desk lording it over a group of Sikh merchants. They stood before him in supplication, negotiating compensation for their burnt properties and monetary losses. The meeting was being presided over by one of Delhi's social/political activists who prided herself as an arbiter of social justice. I lost any semblance of politeness and shouted shame at these Sardars and ordered Bhagat to make himself scarce or come down and face the women. This sight of supplication before one of the alleged perpetrators was an aspect of Sikhhood as completely alien to me, as had been the earlier experience of witnessing at lunchtime a group of Sikhs being segregated from the common eating area. They were, I was informed by one of the 'leaders', Mazhabi Sikhs. Expressing my ignorance of what this meant, I was informed they were harijans. Revolted by this information, I asked him and others whether all of us weren't harijans too? After all, who else converts to another religion other than the 'have nots'? My question remained unanswered. A day earlier I had heard a similarly uninformed comment voicing fear of 'Muslim raj' recurring. When I inquired what they meant, the answer was that Rajiv Gandhi's father Feroze was a Muslim. Never mind that his surname was Gandhi. So flabbergasted was I, that I recounted this to my mother, who said that post-Independence many Sikhs and Hindus felt that Nehru was favouring Muslims because his son in law Feroze was a Muslim, when in truth he was a Parsi.

The day after the H.K.L. Bhagat incident, my uncle, who was an IAS officer in Patna, was informed by a colleague in the Home Ministry that an order of inquiry against me had been instituted because 'they', whoever 'they' might be, thought I was a Marxist student from

Jawaharlal Nehru University. From then on my rah-of Sikh pride or solidarity would always be tarnished by these two incredible and disillusioning memories.

From the seventh day onwards we witnessed that curious Delhi breed of do-gooders make regular visits to the camp. There were those who came bearing truckloads of food-packages, clothes, and other relief material. Once there, notwithstanding our earnest entreaties, they insisted on personally distributing them to the people they described as 'the Destitutes'. More often than not, they were so overwhelmed by the scores of outstretched hands clamouring for any freebies that they hurriedly dumped the food/clothes, and whatever else they may have collected, and sped away as soon as they could. Good deed done. The piles of inappropriate clothing just grew higher and larger, presenting yet another thankless chore to be attended to. Then came the reporters, social scientists, and members of various political parties, from earnest Marxists to zealous RSS cadres. They all had one common agenda, of recording historical 'first person accounts', and with these visitations the hapless inhabitants relived the horror a dozens of times a day in the vain hope that their stories would catalyse into miracles that would magically resurrect their old familiar lives.

I returned home late at night from one such harrowing day to be greeted by my mother, father-in-law, a few friends, and, most important of all, my daughter. Nikhat had insisted on coming home to be with her mother, missing from her young life for over a week. She had refused to sleep and, as soon as she saw me, began screaming with rage. Her despair and bewilderment at all that was 'not right' in her life, of being abandoned, was all encompassed in that scream. She would not let me approach her until I began singing her favourite childhood lullaby. I gathered her into my arms, attempting to evoke a sense of safety. My brave, happy, generous, sunshine daughter who was too young to understand why her Papa was no longer living with her, but nonetheless confused and hurt. Now, into her young life I had added to her sense of abandonment and insecurity by leaving her with my friends and parents. She and her two friends instinctively sensed that at this young age they were being at the centre of and convulsed by a complex emotional crisis. That all their familiar signposts of security were collapsing beneath their feet.

For many years after that, their favourite game was to role-play a victim shouting 'My house is on fire; help me, save me,' and the other two would act as fire engines and the army arriving to rescue her. They externalized their internal fears by turning it into game, the final act of which has a happy ending. For the children in the camps however the final act was one of tragedy.

Amidst of all this sadness, on 12 November a friend's wedding *sangeet* was held. It could not be postponed because his father had recently died and the elders of the family had insisted that the wedding functions should be held on the days specially selected by him. Neither he nor any of his friends or family were in a celebratory mood but we felt we had to rally around them at a time when we were all bravely coping with our own personal bereavements, now fused into a much larger sense of loss.

The evening began late at night with many police check-posts to be navigated en route. That evening is a jumbled recollection of memories as we took solace in a Bacchanalian orgy. Drinking recklessly and singing and dancing to traditional Punjabi songs in a vain attempt to recreate our lives prior to 31 October 1984. There was none amongst us who did not stumble into their beds that night more than half inebriated. Some needed to be hoisted on the shoulders of others to descend the staircase. I remember returning home in the early hours of the morning. As I once again negotiating all those check-posts, I yearned to scream at these custodians of law: 'Where were you on the nights between 31 October and 3 November?' I cried myself asleep, and awoke to another day of misery.

I listened to women and men in the camps, continually wondering why none of their neighbours, the very people with whom they had lived all their lives, had protected them. They had instead in many instances betrayed them, and sometimes led the mob to their houses. Why had only so few of their Hindu friends helped them? Why were there just a handful of stories of neighbours helping Sikh families? Why did my younger brother suddenly find himself, like the Muslims of this country, an unwanted tenant? One landlord actually told him to his face that he did wish his house to be burnt.

By then the riots had spread to 40 cities across India. The final count: 8,000 Sikhs killed across India, 5,000 in Delhi. The only sterling exception was Calcutta where the Marxist government of Jyoti Basu did not allow a single Sikh to be harmed, unlike the 'riots' of 1969 in Ahmedabad where B.N. Pande records that a marauding Hindu mob had burned down all the Hindu shops at the edge of a shanty town but leaving Muslim homes within the colony untouched. Puzzled, he asked the Hindus what had happened. They told him that an armed mob had come from outside and asked them to point out Muslim homes in the *basti* and, when they refused, had threatened to set fire to their shops. They had stood firm, provoking the mob to go on a spree of arson. Pande asked the Hindus why they hadn't protected their livelihoods by simply pointing out the Muslim homes. 'We're all from the same village in Rajasthan,' they told him. 'What face would we have shown back home if we had betrayed our Muslim brethren?' (Masseh Rahman, *Fulcrum*) .

As was to be expected, several films and books, both documentary and fictional, on the Delhi riots were made or written in the following years. The first was H.S. Phoolka's who, together with human rights activist and journalist Manoj Mitta, wrote *When A Tree Shook Delhi*. Notable among other written accounts were Uma Chakravarthi and Nandita Haksar's *The Delhi Riots: Three*

Days in the Life of a Nation, Jarnail Singh's *Accused*, and Kuldip Nayyar and Khushwant Singh's *Tragedy of Punjab: Operation Bluestar and After.* Shonali Bose's film *Amu*, made in 2005, based on her own novel of the same name, won the National Film Award for Best Feature Film in English but was censored, though the DVD version was released without any cuts. Other films that made a major impact were *Kaya Taran* based on a Malayalam short story, *When a Big Tree Falls* by N.S. Madhavan, and *Hawayein* by Babbu Mann and Ammtoje Mann, based on the aftermath of the Sikh riots and the victimization of the people of Punjab in the years that followed.

- 17 -

Rajiv Gandhi

Rajiv Gandhi was sworn in as the sixth prime minister of India on the second day after his mother's death. This was contrary to the precedent in the Congress party that the seniormost member of the government should be sworn in as interim prime minister until Congress members of parliament meet to elect their new leader. Rajiv Gandhi had just been four years in active politics and had held no office in his mother's government. The die of dynastic politics in the Congress party had been cast the day Indira Gandhi had persuaded her reluctant elder son to join the party after the death of his younger brother.

Rajiv's first remark for public consumption at a boat club rally on November (Indira Gandhi's birthday) virtually justified the massacre of over 5,000 Sikhs:

Rajiv Gandhi's first address to the nation after being sworn in, as Prime Minister, Delhi, 1984 (Courtesy: PIB).

‘Some riots took place in the country following the murder of Indiraji. We know that the people are very angry and for a few days it seemed India is shaken. But when a mighty tree falls it is only natural that the earth around it does shake a little.’ We were stupefied by what we heard. At the time some of us were still visiting the camps and it certainly did not appear to us to have only been a faint tremor of the earth. We subsequently learnt that the speech had been written by one of his devoted cronies. Even so, that did not by any means justify our youngest ever prime minister, still in deep mourning, describing the deaths of over 8,000 people as ‘some riots’. If his mother was murdered so were all the relatives of these disenfranchised citizens of India. That evening, a concert was organized at Pragati Maidan where all the leading classical singers participated to pay homage to the assassinated leader. Tellingly, each of them made Indira Gandhi the entire focus of the event, paying little or no attention to the enormous tragedy that followed which brutally destroyed thousands of lives in retaliation. While it was ironically a reminder of the pitfalls of personality politics, hubris and its inevitable outcome, it was also a pointer to the shortsightedness of human nature. Rajiv's subsequent election campaign posters depicted a bearded man behind barbed wire with the caption 'Know your enemy'. These were certainly not positive indications of a man driven by any sense of justice for all.

Rajiv had however been thrust into a position he had not sought or anticipated. To his credit, he threw himself into it with an innocence and faith in his own capacity to carry India forward. His personal goals, which were not diluted by political expediency, succeeded. Most tangible was his technology mission through which he introduced India to the wonders and powers of a digital world, with the eventual aim of bringing telecommunications to every citizen's door. I remember the thrill at seeing STD booths in almost every village we passed on my travels relating to development work. The information technology revolution that has gripped India (and the world) today owes its daring beginnings to Rajiv.

Early in his term it was he who pushed forward the Assam accord, the short-lived Longowal accord, and the call for elections in Punjab in 1985. He was deeply committed to introducing Panchayati Raj or democracy at the grass roots. Most Indians were willing to support him in achieving his core developmental goals. These translated into: job creation, increased opportunities for self-employment, support of small entrepreneurs, egalitarian local self-government, cutting down the practice of the licence raj, holding bureaucrats accountable, educational reforms. For many he was India's dream prime minister and the majority was willing to give him benefit of doubt. To excuse his laxity in not having ordered immediate restoration of calm and law and order following his mother's death. They believed that he was still a novice and his good intentions should be honoured. That he would soon understand the complex synergy of politics where every word must be carefully weighed times before being uttered. A friend of mine, the daughter of a veteran politician from Uttar Pradesh, remarked, 'If he has entered politics then someone should advise him to keep his enemies in front of him and his friends behind him'.

Very soon after taking over office he advised the president to dissolve parliament and hold general elections. The people of India voted him and the Congress in with the largest majority ever in the history of Indian parliamentary elections to date: 411 seats

Rajiv Gandhi with his entourage , Delhi 1984 (Courtesy: PIB).

out a total of 542. We were by now ready to forgive his initial insensitivity as the aberration of a grieving and ill-prepared son.

His first speech on the environment, a hot topic with activists and voluntary organizations, floored even his most vigorous critics. Some of my friends and colleagues emerged jubilantly from Vigyan Bhawan after having heard their young prime minister address all the key issues concerning forest protection, the debate between large dam projects and displacement, and other allied issues in a daze of admiring disbelief. Developmental challenges were apparently no longer insurmountable and they all pledged unstinting support. This was particularly so because one of his concluding observations was that he was well aware that for every rupee allocated by the government for the poor, 90 paise was pocketed by the official machinery responsible for administering the people-oriented programmes. He appealed to the voluntary sector to help him, and promised that he in turn would ensure that their goals and objectives were achieved. These were men and women like him. Most had spurned the opportunity of lucrative jobs, opting, after their education in premium institutions in India and abroad, to serve the people. To work for a greener, more equitable India with provisions for health, education, and equal opportunities for all. We had our own Camelot. No one looked deeper into the debacle of the original Camelot or the one closer to our time in the Kennedy years.

The voluntary sector had always been viewed by the

establishment as an adversarial force and had overnight been promised the approval and support of the prime minister. A leader who was more willing to listen to their version of the ground realities than to those set out by his officers. The larger NGOs were challenged to run parallel government-sponsored programmes rather than continue in their traditional role as catalysts between the people and the government. This encouraged smaller ones to follow suit. However, in their eagerness to support the prime minister's vision, they established large infrastructures which tied them to insupportable financial budgets. This caused them to become forever beholden to central/state government financial aid and subservient to foreign funders and foundations. NGOs were represented in the Planning Commission and in state level planning bodies but had ceased to work on pilot development projects. The learning gained from these and any success achieved would have fed into similar large government programmes. The NGO sector, because they believed in Rajiv's direction, were amenable to redefining their role in the developmental process.

The country, especially Delhi, was once again infused with the spirit of nation building witnessed by the earlier two generations under the stewardship of Rajiv's grandfather, Jawaharlal Nehru, and during his mother's the first five-year term. We would constantly hear a murmur of approval from the older generation. They dared to hope that their struggles would be rewarded, even though, during the second phase of Indira Gandhi's prime-ministership, even my mother and others, staunch supporters of her. felt she had lost her moral compass.

•

During his first year in office Rajiv Gandhi was faced with enormous tragedies, the first among them the horrific industrial disaster, one of the world's worst, at the Union Carbide factory in Bhopal. This horrific event took place on the morning of 3 December 1984 but we of course were blissfully unaware of it. The news reached Delhi that thousands of men, women, and children had died vainly fleeing from a cloud of poisonous gas. Nobody seemed to know exactly what had happened. There had been an accident at the Union Carbide Corporation's pesticide factory where water had leaked into a gas tank and it had exploded. Many of us in Saheli had friends and family living in Bhopal. Everyone was frantic to learn how they were. As the day wore on we heard of dead bodies lying in the streets and no one knew the nature of the poisonous gas. It emerged that the gas cloud might contain phosgene, hydrogen cyanide, carbon monoxide, and many other elements. Only months later was the gas identified as Methyl Isocyanate (MIC) along with other chemicals

There was widespread concern as people were reporting a burning sensation in their eyes, and those who had run the fastest to escape had suffered most. People were awaiting information from the government which they themselves did not have. In a day or two civil society was demanding that the UCC management should be criminally prosecuted. News leaked out that the management had received many warnings/had experienced previous accidents, but had not heightened their safety regulations. Neither the state or national governments had the necessary information to help the affected people. All of us were in a state of shock, not knowing what to do.

Warren Anderson, the chairman of UCC, flew down to Delhi at a time when people were consumed with rage. The government apparently placed him under house arrest but before any real help was provided to the affected people he was flown out of the country in order not to jeopardize India's future business interests. (This was also believed to be in exchange for the release of Muhammad Yunus's son from an American prison. Muhammad Yunus was a Gandhi family friend and confidante whose last claim to fame during the Emergency had been to instruct the CBI director to soundly spank Mark Tully of the BBC for speaking and writing against it.) We could scarcely believe what was happening. The government, to prevent people from filing criminal and compensation cases against the company, negotiated a settlement with the UCC for $450 m. in compensation, a woefully inadequate sum and a pittance in comparison with the compensation that such an accident would have entailed in the US. All these years later, many affected people continue to struggle for justice and compensation for their injuries and the site still remains toxic.

It was several months later that Saheli members joined a medical team visiting Bhopal to study the impact of MIC on pregnant women and newborn babies. We walked around the *bastis* fringing the company complex and saw the agony of pregnant women who could barely breathe. Painstakingly we recorded their health condition. We also attempted to meet women who had miscarried during the days following the incident. A team of 40 women worked together with doctors to assess the situation. Most of the poor were already malnourished and the exposure to MIC had further devastated them. It was subsequently established that stillbirths had risen by 300 per cent and neonatal mortality by 200 per cent.

•

Notwithstanding the Bhopal tragedy, we were all confident that Rajiv was determined to deliver on his campaign promises. Even the opposition parties were willing to support him as he believed in inclusiveness, their support by inviting debate and consensus in parliament: 'Just like his grandfather,' was a remark frequently heard in the corridors of power.

Most of us who were involved in aspects of development were riding a slightly bumpy euphoric wave. We believed that we were finally in charge of our personal destinies and the nation's, and these were precisely the opportunities that we had been awaiting. We were the natural heirs of our grandparents' and parents' legacies, and the onus was on us to carry forward their vision and sacrifice. We, along with millions of Indians of our generation, would succeed in making Mahatma Gandhi's vision a reality. Rajiv Gandhi surrounded himself with some of the most intelligent minds of his generation, among them a few of his close friends from school and university who shared a common vision for their country. His greatest asset, and those of his handpicked advisors, was a reputation for incorruptibility.

Alas, governance and politics require a more complex set of skills where the operational colour is shades of grey. Incorruptibility is just one of the criteria. Experience, expediency, and the ability to sense and deflect potential threats are prerequisites for the task. The early tremor which created a crack in the walls of Camelot had been the mismanagement of the Bhopal gas tragedy. Nonetheless, a majority of Indians continued to believe in their young prime minister. Then came two catastrophic interventions by the government which would have serious implications for the future of secularism in India.

History is replete with anecdotes of minor ripples that eventually churn into tidal waves, destroying in their path precious values and principles that are the guiding framework of all that we hold dear. Shah Bano, a Muslim woman from a small town in Uttar Pradesh, could never in her wildest imagination have dreamt of the repercussions of her decision to demand, under civil law, the maximum yet paltry maintenance of Rs 500 from her husband who had divorced her under Muslim personal law. It was to gravely threaten the fabric of secularism enshrined in the Constitution. When accepting her appeal and granting a judgment in her favour, Justice V.Y. Chandrachud added a few observations on Muslim personal law which were regarded by the religious heads of the faith as being insulting to the faith. The significance of this was revealed by the mass demonstrations organized in Uttar Pradesh and Delhi led by the Muslim clergy. These, apart from creating a law and order situation, seriously concerned veteran Congress leaders as indicative of a meltdown of the party's so called Muslim vote bank.

It was for us in Saheli and the women's movement a historic judgment in setting a precedent for other not so well to do women, especially the poor. The debate reached parliament and was eagerly observed from the visitors' gallery by concerned visitors and activists who had lobbied hard for parliament to support the judgement. We all waited with bated breath for our prime minister to resist the pressure from the party and the Muslim religious community and defend the judgement. Arif Muhammad Khan, his minister who was to debate the issue, spoke passionately, eloquently, quoting from the Hadith and Sharia in its defence, assuming that this was what his leader wished him to do. However, around midnight a day earlier, Rajiv Gandhi had been persuaded to present an alternative bill. His advisers had argued that it would be political hara-kiri to accept the judgement, and an alternative bill, *The Muslim Women (Protection of Rights on Divorce) Act 1986* was introduced instead and passed. (The Act stipulated that even destitute Muslim divorcees would not be entitled to such maintenance from the husband after the period known as *iddat*.) No one outside a tight inner circle of advisors was aware of this. Arif Mohammad Khan was caught as unaware as the rest of us and promptly resigned from the Congress.

The second more momentous decision with disastrous consequences which will affect generations of

Indians was to order the UP government to unlock the gates to the makeshift Ram Mandir in Ayodhya. This had been surreptitiously constructed within the Babri Masjid, and had been ordered to be locked by the court while the case remained subjudice. This decision was arrived at on the advice of the staunch Hindu wing within the Congress party which felt that a grand gesture was now needed to be made to the Hindus who were chafing at the perceived appeasement of Muslims. Until then only a priest had been permitted to perform puja once a year to the idols installed there in 1949. With the unlocking of Ram Mandir all Hindus were permitted to worship there. Physically this did not alter the mosque with a makeshift temple within it but it fundamentally altered the political, social, and religious underpinnings of the site. No one had thought through the decision, and it led to the widespread belief that Rajiv Gandhi was favouring the Hindu claim to the site. To compound matters, Rajiv Gandhi in 1989 sanctioned the *shilanyas* ceremony during which the first stone of a temple proposed to be built there was put in place amidst much fanfare.

Again, in 1986, sedition charges were levelled against the editor of the *Economic and Political Weekly* by the Bombay police. The reason cited was an article by a contributor on the alleged atrocities on civilians in Amritsar by the army in the aftermath of Operation Bluestar. However, the disastrous repercussions of Rajiv's actions on his own image and image of the country abroad were fortuitously pointed out to the prime minister by a professor representing the views of a majority of the intelligentsia, and Rajiv instructed the chief minister of the state to drop the charges. This was a clear example of the ease with which an order from the high command could rescind the orders of a chief minister.

These errors of judgement were further exposed and exacerbated when Rajiv's Gandhi's defence minister, V.P. Singh, levelled serious charges of corruption against the government in the Bofors case concerning the purchase of Swedish howitzers for the army. He resigned in protest against the charges not being properly investigated.

Why? was a perpetual question on all our lips. Evenings in Delhi buzzed and sometimes exploded with arguments and counter-arguments on how these sharp fissures in India's secular fabric could be repaired. Had it not been for that one singular act in Ayodhya, to this day the VHP and other Hindu fundamentalist organizations and the more moderate face of the BJP would still be campaigning to have the Ram Mandir unlocked. This would have circumvented the riots, arson, and mayhem, especially in Bombay, following the destruction of the Babri Masjid. The Congress's appeasement strategies, apart from being indicative of the party's inability to govern, displayed a lack of confidence in themselves. This was amply illustrated in the ridiculous decision to ban Salman Rushdie's *The Satanic Verses* in order to stop Syed Shahbuddin's protest march of Muslims in 1988 against the Ayodhya decision.

- 18 -

Amidst the Cultural Mainstream

Many of us were simultaneously living several lives, energized by the belief that we would, despite all the odds, succeed in our goals. This, even after discovering that our very own King Arthur had been discovered to have feet of clay. At a personal level, I had reconciled myself to bidding farewell to B, my own knight in shining armour.

By a curious quirk of fate I was married and divorced on the same day: 9 December 1973 and 9 December 1987. I viewed this as a sign that one more phase of my life had run its full circle. It felt unreal to be going to Tees Hazari Court for my own divorce, having on innumerable occasions escorted other women with far fewer options than mine. Ours was a divorce by mutual consent. My bargaining chip was that B should transfer bureaucrats, environmentalists, musicians, theatre actors, architects, and those in publishing. We would greedily and vociferously share our experiences, and read suggested books. I felt that I was once more reliving my Delhi University years as a member of a very special group which shared a common ideology. Sometimes even a perceived change within the core ideals would lead to passionate debates with tempers rising, aided by the time of the night and quantity of alcohol consumed. We were like the 'pack brats' except that we were not indulgent or destructive, although some of us were seriously on the road to living with damaged livers.

The years 1987–88 ushered in a period of acute drought in many states of northern India. My trips to remote villages of Rajasthan, especially in the Jaisalmer-Barmer belt and the adivasi areas of Gujarat left me completely shattered. I was witness to the break-up of families. This was because village after village had been deserted by the able-bodied who perforce had to migrate to cities for sustenance, leaving their aged and infirm parents to manage on their dwindling stock of rations. The only heartening experiences were in the Bishnoi villages where the tradition of offering water to animals

Heady times. Delhi, mid-80s (Courtesy: Suman Dubey).

At a friend's 40th birthday party, attired á la the 1940s, bar the cigar.

and birds continued. Here the community would walk many kilometres to harvest it from ponds and wells choked with algae. On one of my trips they insisted that I walk with them to show me the water source. When we arrived, they offered me a scoop of it. Much as my system recoiled, I drank it out of respect, reassuring myself that if the tiny frogs I could see in it were alive, so would I survive.

Most evenings with friends were spent passionately debating the cause and effect of skewed developmental programmes. The apparently pro-poor budgets which were in reality the reverse. The rise of religious fundamentalism, the Punjab militant crisis. We also l debated the recurring short-sightedness of central government policies in the North-East and Jammu & Kashmir. We convinced ourselves that our enlightened prime minister and his team of able advisors were being stymied by the 'Old Guard'. The evenings would end with all of us on the dance floor. We no longer danced to familiar western rock groups or the classics of yesteryear, but instead to the classics of the Hindi film world. At the top of the list was invariably Kishore Kumar. This was an import into Delhi from Calcutta friends, certainly lowbrow for the snob Delhi set, but very infectious and seductive.

Returning home late at night was always a hazard because New Delhi's landscape was now dotted with numerous check-posts. Burly men with AK 47s carelessly hanging from their shoulders, peering into our cars, and randomly questioning people. Such tactics were a laughable way of eliciting nuggets of information on 'militant movements', as they called it, before they waved us on. One particularly embarrassing night is etched in my memory. A friend who was staying with me insisted I stop the car immediately as she needed to throw up. When I did, a shower of Vodka/Campari mix spewed out, just eluding the polished boots of one such burly figure.

In the early 1990s there were the underground parties, the brainchild of some of my gay friends. It all began with the 'red rose' evenings in a coffee house on the roof of a commercial building called Mohan Singh Place. Wedged between Rivoli Cinema and Hanuman Mandir on the outer edge of Connaught Place, this NDMC construction stood out like a sore thumb. The communists had adopted the Coffee House as their *adda*. If I ever wanted to meet my uncle and his friends outside my parents' home this was where I was certain to find him in the company of a group of old diehard journalists. They, as the sun set over the roofs of Lutyens's Delhi, would move to their favourite watering hole, the Press Club on Raisina Road, on a hill that the British had earmarked as the centre of their own capital, New Delhi. Ironical that the lefties had appropriated a small corner of the last vestige of the British Empire.

For the gay community, the coffee house signalled

perhaps the first emergence of the movement, timorous and tentative. The tables, indicating safety and acceptability, would have a red rose placed on them. Members of this hush-hush club, which gradually grew to include not only the 'fancies' (élite members who could lay claim to education abroad) but the 'vernies' or so called 'vernacular' types, among whom were rickshaw-pullers and others. Language was a clear divide but they were invited to pick up each other's roses and proceed to spend a pleasurable evening together.

I was, for a few of my gay friends, the token woman, and would be invited not to the coffee house but to these underground parties. We would travel all over Delhi, from a bungalow in the army cantonment, duly guarded by uniformed subedars, to places in trans-Jamuna. That is, anywhere from Golf Links to New Rajinder Place where the party was planned. This was for me the single most liberating experience post the break-up of my marriage. I did not do the most predictable ego massage: start an affair with one of the several men who suddenly seemed more attentive, but found my mojo by safely and uninhibitedly dancing with strange gay men or just by myself. There was no 'danger' lurking in the shadows. No judgements, no fuss, no 'I need to be careful with that man'. Just pure fun. Young and not so young men from all walks of life, even the young 'gaylets' from college, still uncertain about their sexual inclinations, would all happily greet one another and dance. The lesbian representation was in a minority. I will always recall a particular evening when we were invited to an engagement party of a gay friend who was besotted by a beautiful young man and announced they were getting engaged. They came from different cultures, background, and class, but none of that mattered. I sat with one of my girlfriends, most envious of the young man's emerald and diamond art deco bracelets gifted by my friend, his fiance. We noticed that our group was being singled out by the young man's brother and served the choicest kababs, while my girlfriend kept whispering that the elder brother looked very familiar. Suddenly she clutched my hand and exclaimed. 'Oh my God, he is my butcher in Malviya Nagar.'We straddled what appeared to be totally different planets in each 24 hour day, one as comfortable as the other.

The theatre world had once more awoken to the political/social changes that beset it. Street theatre became an established form of communication, especially post the Safdar Hashmi murder. Groups like Astaha and Allaripu became well known for their social commentary on oppression and divisive politics.

Following the searing post-Partition plays produced by the Indian Peoples Theatre Association (IPTA) and the Prithviraj Kapoor theatre group starring, among others, the two Sehgal sisters (Zohra and Uzra), came the Kendalls. Their Shakespereana travelled the length and breadth of India bringing the English bard's plays alive for schoolchildren. These were followed by Sheila Bhatia's Punjabi operas, reliving the rich tapestry of Punjab for the broken refugees of Partition. How could we ever forget the haunting love story of *Heer Ranjha* with Shanno Khurana in the lead role. The language of theatre was becoming more frequent in the vernacular with Hindi, Punjabi, Sanskrit, and Bengali dominating the Delhi theatre scene. This was another awakening in our convent-educated upbringing.

At the same time, English theatre was making a resurgence with Yatrik and the Theatre Action Group (TAG). The latter with the young Barry John and his highly dedicated and talented actors who trained with him and stayed with the group. *Waiting for Godot* and *Equus* were two of his iconic productions during this phase. Shahrukh Khan, Mira Nair, and Khalid Tayabji were among his stars. Theatre received its biggest push with the entry of Ebrahim Alkazi and the establishment of the National School of Drama. Over the years its repertory company distinguished itself with productions that were much awaited and never disappointed. Its lead actors became household names to us, by then, theatre-hungry Delhiites: Manohar Singh, Surekha Sikri, Uttara Baokar, to be followed by younger talents such as Naseeruddin Shah, Om Puri, and others. *Tughlaq* was magnificently staged at Purana Qila, as was *Andha Yug*. Classics of Indian drama along with translations of more modern Western plays had us starry-eyed. From the north-east of India came Rattan Thiyam, mesmerizing us with his *Chakyravyuh*. The distance between Bombay, the only cosmopolitan city, Calcutta, the cultural capital, and Delhi was closing. We looked forward to Tendulkar's productions from Bombay, memorable among them being *Ghasiram Kotwal*, as much as to Habib Tanveer's vernacular political satires based in the folklore of tribal Chhattisgarh in Madhya Pradesh. His *Charan Das Chor*,

Raja Ka Sala, and *Agra Bazaar* were restaged repeatedly in response to incessant demand from ardent fans.

In the fine arts there seemed to be a spontaneous shift from the abstract style of modern art to the narrative. Experimentation with folk traditions, archiving indigenous trades, portraying the common man, creating human forms that were vivid and real. Figure rooted in enormous despair and disillusionment, and occasional movement into pop culture. The emerging new heroes from Maharashtra were Bhupen Khakhar, Ghulam Sheikh, and others, questioning and turning raw life, such as the Baroda riots, into pictorial narratives. In Bombay, Nalini Malani was inspired by the ironsmiths below her studio. Then there were the suggestive figurative works of Gieve Patel, Arpita Singh, Jogen Chowdhury, Vivan Sundaram, Manjit Bawa, and Swaminathan. Arpita Singh's post 1984 paintings clearly reflected her inner ability to absorb the violence and destruction surrounding her and transfer it on to her canvas as if the subconscious was taking a hold on reality. Her painting of a mother crossing the street to undertake everyday chores, blind to the riots on the right of the street, will remain with me forever. Many of the artists portrayed the corrupt nature of our politicians, the greed of industrialists, emoting powerful messages of broken promises. Artists like Jatin Das engaged with the nature of the man-woman relationship. Some portrayed repressed sexuality, with subtle but sure brushstrokes of homo-eroticism and sexual liberation. At the same time they were crafting and painting a brave new world, optimistic of the possibility of renewal. They were the bridge between the Modern and the new age Digital Art of the mid-1990s.

The world of classical Indian music and dance was also breaking out of the preserve of the legendary dynasties. We could easily relate to Amjad Ali Khan, closer to our generation, but class distinctions were getting blurred. We were excited to attend the concerts of Biswajeet Roychowdhury, an exceptional sarod player, and Buddhadev Mukherjee, both rising stars with non-musical backgrounds.

Similarly, Alarmel Valli and Malvika Sarukkai, the two young stars of Bharatanatyam, were, like their predecessor Yamini Krishnamurthy, not from a tradition of dance and music. Kathak, the classical dance form of north India, was taking its cue from theatre and developing into highly choreographed performances.

In the film world, we had all been awed by Satyajit Ray's classic *Apu* trilogy (1950s-60s) and his pioneering style was echoed in the new wave cinema of realism of the 1970s and '80s by directors such as Kumar Shahani, Mani Kaul, M.S. Sathyu, Shyam Benegal, Saeed Mirza, and others. They boldly questioned issues concerning the state, human rights, politics, national history, and the idea of India. In the south, Adoor Gopalakrishnan was a big name for us and an entire crop of young stars became our heroes and heroines: Shabana Azmi, Smita Patil, Om Puri, Amol Palekar. Shakuntalam, a tiny cinema hall at Pragati Vihar had become a mecca for those of us who had become entranced by the films of Bergman, Eisenstein, Tarkovsky, Truffaut, Goddard, and others through the film clubs run by the cultural centres of the various embassies and the occasional film festivals they organized. The tickets there were inexpensive and the fare both popular and unexpected, and, especially when trade fares were being organized, there were post-film eateries as bonus: 'cheap and best'.

We were all monetarily stretched to meet our monthly bills, but felt rich in our exposure to creativity

Celebrating Holi at Alka Dalmia's house Delhi, 1985 (Courtesy: Suman Dubey).

and our determination to merge our individual identities in the larger collective of 'our kind of people, our dream India'.

- 19 -

Nine Green Bottles and the Janata Dal

I have often asked my friends whether V.P. Singh was destiny's child or Sanjay Gandhi's second big mistake. The first chink in the armour of Sanjay's almost foolproof political survival instinct was Sant Bhinderwale and the second was Vishvanath Pratap Singh, the Rajah of Manda.

The story goes that Sanjay Gandhi wanted a young, energetic, pliant chief minister for Uttar Pradesh rather than a member of the Congress old guard. V.P. Singh fitted the bill to a nicety and became Sanjay's point man. Later, like many others of Sanjay's inner coterie, he also found favour in Rajiv Gandhi's cabinet in 1985. Perhaps appointing him Defence Minister was a misjudgement on Rajiv's part because V.P. Singh, defending India's moral fibre, focused on multimillion kickbacks in defence deals. In his accusations of gross financial impropriety relating to the HDW submarine purchase deal and, later, the infamous Bofors howitzer deal, our evangelist found his true calling: fighting corruption at the highest levels. V.P. Singh took to the media like a duck to water by bringing out into the open uncomfortable facts allegedly involving Rajiv Gandhi. For this audacity he was eventually dismissed from the Congress. He launched a new political party called Jan Morcha in 1987 with a one point programme: fighting corruption. He triumphed in the Allahabad bye-election, winning the seat vacated by Amitabh Bachchan (who had soon tired of politics) and took to the road like a true blue crusader. Flourishing his symbolic sword of incorruptibility' and gathering momentum as he toured India, he attracted gullible crowds who soon began viewing him as their saviour.

He formed the Janata Dal in 1988, merging Jan Morcha with Chandrashekar's Janata Party, the Lok Dal, and Congress (S). The new party was viewed by the people at large as the panacea for all the ills of the corruption bedevilling it. Strategic calculations necessitated a coalition with the National Front, a melange of regional parties, and an electoral understanding with the Communists and the BJP. These 'nine green bottles' had once more banded together with a single point agenda of defeating the Congress in the 1989 elections. The Congress however emerged as the single largest party with 197 seats, but declined to form a government with outside support. The Janata Dal, led by V.P. Singh, won 143 seats, and the BJP with 85 and were the largest gainers; in the 8th Lok Sabha elections they had won only two seats. The Left parties won 45 seats.

V.P. Singh became the prime minister of the National Front government and Devi Lal the deputy prime minister, bypassing Chandrashekar's claim with deft manipulations. The game of nine green bottles sitting on the wall began on the day the government was sworn in. History never ever seems to teach individuals, communities, the country, and specifically politicians, any lessons. My friends and I despaired as the repeat button played the old Janata Party song, or should I say, dirge, of ambitions, egos, mistrust, and disloyalty. Politically, the militant crisis in Kashmir had worsened with a large-scale migration of Hindu Kashmiris out of the valley. With every crisis the BJP was consolidating the Hindu vote under the Ram Mandir banner.

Faced with internal and international crises, V.P. Singh pulled the Mandal card from his magic hat to consolidate the 'backward' vote in his favour and on 7 August 1990, ordered the implementation of the Mandal report in entirety. All hell broke loose in the Hindi heartland and in the middle and upper echelons of Delhi society. There were explosions of largely middle-class anger, fuelled by both a sense of entitlement and fear in many parts of India. Young students, backed by their parents, took to the streets. They claimed they were fighting for a level playing field with merit as the sole criterion, for justice, and for their rights as students. They staged dharnas, faced lathi charges, and fought pitched battles with the police, possibly for the first time since the struggle for India's independence. Parents unabashedly expressed apprehension that their children would now no longer be able to enjoy the full benefits of education. That they would not get the jobs to which they felt they were entitled on the basis of 'merit', never mind that some of this 'merit' had been made possible by virtue of birth.

Delhi's students protesting against the Mandal recommendations (Courtesy: Hindustan Times).

Delhi was foremost in spearheading the agitation. The socially and politically correct chatterati class spewing venom against V.P. Singh in particular, and the Janata Dal government in general. Lovers of Balraj Sahni and Raj Kapoor's popular yet searing movies about our Motherland's economic and social underdogs and the callous cruelty and fetid indignity of their lives, saw no irony in openly agitating against a relatively small step taken to set right ancient wrongs. To bring some semblance of equity in our caste-ridden society.

A close friend of mine was then a young minister in the V.P. Singh government with a variety of friends from school, college, and previous professional days, and of course from the world of politics. The hot topic of discussion during the ongoing agitation was the newly implemented policy on reservations. What however took my friend and his wife aback was the vitriolic verbal attack by friends and strangers alike on 'your government's decision'. The vehemence of the discussion at numerous social gatherings, its 'us' versus 'them' character, the lack of empathy for the less privileged, the misinformation and complete ignorance of the reality of the entrenched casteism rampant in Indian communities in large parts of India, was shocking.

Many said, 'V.P. Singh has brought caste into our lives'; our children didn't even know which caste they belonged to until V.P. Singh brought in Reservations'. 'Lucky children they' is all I can say. It was as if Bindheshwari Prasad Mandal had invented caste and villainous V.P. Singh had breathed life into it. 'Who is Manu; what is *Manusmriti*'? If their ignorance (feigned or otherwise) didn't make me grind my teeth and choke over my much-needed drink, I would have been amused.

V.P. Singh at a reception in the Maldive Islands, 1990.

During this period there were a number of very tragic suicides by students. All of them, without proper investigation, were linked to the student agitation against the Mandal reservations, and they became martyrs to the cause. The media — largely newspapers, apart from a couple of nascent private news programmes — depicted each suicide as the ultimate glorious sacrifice for the cause. This, tragically, appeared to encourage (according to sociologists) copycat suicides.

V.P. Singh's Mandal card unexpectedly brought caste identity centrestage and developed a keener awareness of caste identities among Hindus. The Mandal agitation was the cue for Lal Krishan Advani's closet Pied Piper to make a dramatic 'coming out' statement. He jumped on to a modern-day version of the *rath* with a resounding battlecry, '*Garv se bolo hum Hindu hain*', causing many of us to justifiably inquire what they had been up to now. His *rath yatra* was a clarion cry to all Hindus of various hues of saffron to literally jump on the bandwagon. This was their holy war, and to the resounding cries of '*Har Har Mahadev*' they set off on their journey from Somnath towards Ayodhya, gathering en route hordes of bemused volunteers mesmerized by the Pied Piper. I suspect many young disgruntled jobless youth, having tasted 'blood' à la Mandal, viewed this splendid march to Ayodhya as a ticket to a free meal because whenever the Pied Piper called a halt, his hordes of followers would sit down to a hearty free meal, There young studs proudly flexing their muscles, spurred by the recognition of their prowess. They moved like a cloud of locusts, leaving in their wake a wasteland of hatred. They reinforced biases against non-Hindus, were intolerant of their of own scheduled castes, and belligerent towards other Hindus who were vocally critical of their modus operandi. The yatra generated communal tension in many of the states through which it passed, creating law and order situations. This was the coming of age moment for Pracharak Narendra Damodardas Modi who spearheaded the organization of the Gujarat leg of the *rath yatra.* He did this with such resounding success that he was perceived for the rest of the serpentine journey as the first among equals. He was well-rewarded by Advani who championed his candidature as chief minister of Gujarat and catapulted him to the highest rung of the national BJP edifice. The most telling warning issued by L.K. Advani to V.P. Singh was that were he to be arrested the BJP would withdraw support to his government. We felt totally helpless in the face of this locust-like invasion. Some of my journalist friends kept repeating that 'personally L.K. Advani is a good man'. As a feminist I believed 'the personal is the political' and disagreed with them.

The competitive tussle between Mulayam Singh Yadav, chief minister of Uttar Pradesh, and Lalu Prasad Yadav, chief minister of Bihar, on who would arrest Lal Krishan Advani eventually ended with Lalu Yadav ordering his arrest at Samastipur. The yatra was stopped on 23 October 1990 and the BJP promptly withdrew their outside support to the government. At this juncture, three green bottles accidentally fell.

Meanwhile, Chandrashekar and Devi Lal left the Janata Dal with their 64 MPs to form the Samajwadi Janata Party (Rashtriya) on 5 November 1990. With this, four green bottles accidentally fell. V.P. Singh lost the vote of confidence in the Lok Sabha on 7 November, 1990 and had to resign. Seven green bottles accidentally fell.

Chandrashekar became the prime minister with 'outside support' from the Congress, inherited an economy in a parlous condition, rising prices of essential

L.K. Advani performing a pooja prior to his Rath Yatra (Courtesy: Hindustan Times).

commodities, and foreign exchange reserves falling to dangerously low levels. The country almost slipped into the list of 'debt defaulters' and its image fell worldwide. Like a good Indian housewife, he had to pledge the gold reserves of the country to 'manage the situation'.

Rajiv Gandhi withdrew support to Chandrashekar on 6 March 1991 on the flimsy ground that two police constables had been spying on him, and with that fell all nine green bottles.

- 20 -

Elections Yet Again and Rajiv Gandhi's Assassination

Elections again. The cynics among us shrugged their shoulders and said, 'Well, it's a foolproof way to launder money'. It is only too well known that unaccounted money, euphemistically termed 'donations', usually finds a 'white' home in the coffers of political parties during this period. This outpouring of 'charity' is the general practice among industrialists, entrepreneurs, and whoever else is dependent on government patronage or their political godfathers. Each party as a whole, and also individual candidates, are critically assessed, not just for their current box office appeal but also their potential to develop into powerful leaders in the future. We call it '*lambey daur ka ghoda*' in Hindi, that is, a horse with the potential to win a long race, or many races. The amounts donated are based on a fine balance between rationality and a long-term racing hunch.

Election time is also party time for the printing industry, from producers of sophisticated posters, leaflets, and flyers to the local small town photocopier churning out the humble *aam aadmi* variety. During this period, the profits of petty businesses suddenly soar, beginning with the local chai-wallahs and roadside dhabas, where most of the city-slicker journalists *maro adda* to ferret gossip about the direction in which the wind is blowing before rushing back to file in their daily stories. Here gossip passes off as the 'voice of the rural classes'. Sophisticated English-speaking journalists with anglicized Hindi accents sit on hard, wooden benches at streetside dhabas, part of a team of locusts ready to devour every word uttered by the 'locals'. The latter in turn bask in their moment of glory, puffed up at the attention they are receiving from women journalists, some of whom are as glamorous as Bollywood stars. The automobile industry, through their agents, rent out fleets of jeeps and sturdy second-hand cars, gambling their resources in the fond expectation that they will recoup and multiply their investments. Companies renting out helicopters and small planes are equally vulnerable with bill payments woefully delayed and sometimes irrecoverable, especially if the customer loses the election. The consumption of alcohol too, be it 'English wine and beer' or the local brews, rises astronomically. This is particularly so a day prior to the election when candidates generously distribute booze amongst the electorate. This is a practice that cuts across all parties. At election time, prostitution too is on an ascendancy, as is the sale of sugar-cane (if in season), peanuts, paan, and cigarettes. Local shops in villages and small towns, replete with fresh stocks of all that might conceivably be sold to the itinerant city-slicker, make a killing.

Further up the class ladder, the drawing rooms of Delhi are abuzz with political pundits predicting winners and losers. Sonorous pronouncements are made, are argued and counter-argued. Each 'expert' is smug about his or her own deductive powers and their secret network of contacts providing 'unique' insight. Lesser mortals who consider themselves prescient immediately claim ownership of these pearls of wisdom and pass on what they've heard at yet another political soirée. Subsequent deniability is a key ingredient in such predictions. All this is happening even while politicians and king-makers, in cahoots with members of India Inc., plot, plan, cut, and realign their candidates to enable post-election mobility. This is enacted with a suppleness that permits the candidates in question to pledge total loyalty to the triumphant party without appearing to be opportunists or hypocrites.

Once the results are out, if the margins of the key contenders are small, the chests of independent candidates or those from small regional parties suddenly swell. They are smugly drunk in the knowledge that they now wield the power to make or break a government. The moves resemble tight, overlapping games of chess. Elections and their aftermath are also a bonanza time for godmen and astrologers. Candidates are at this time most inclined to rush to them for blessings, advice, and to order ring upon ring studded with an auspicious gem which will complement their *rashi* or tame their inimical stars. I'm convinced there is a complete understanding of profit sharing between the astrologer and the jeweller: the Brahmin is too wily not to extract his pound of flesh from the Bania.

Closer to the field of play, the constituency, the

local leaders of the various political parties don their Gandhi caps and/or flourish party flags and strut around aware that without their support the prospects of their candidates' winning are minimal. Infighting rules the day. Tried and tested methods of siphoning election funds into the personal accounts of local fixers are deployed, regardless of the eventual outcome. The Mahila Brigade is just as voracious with their large plastic handbags tucked underarm, powdered, coiffed, ready to fight off anyone trespassing on their turf.

•

The stage was thus set for the general elections of May 1991, almost six months prior to the Chief Election Commissioner's announcement that 20, 23, and 26 May would be polling days. People were tired, disillusioned, and ready for a change of government. Their disappointment in particular was with yesterday's hero, V.P. Singh. The Congress, led by Rajiv Gandhi, was making waves wherever he went. He had set himself a gruelling campaign schedule, which set the tempo for the rest of the Congress candidates. People spontaneously flocked to hear him, waiting patiently, sometimes for hours, because he had been delayed by surging crowds reluctant to let go of him. They gathered close to him striving to catch his attention, a nightmare for his meagre squad of security personnel. The elders in the crowd would mutter approvingly that he was just like his grandfather. Most of us who had been critical of what was popularly termed dynastic politics agreed that he had learnt from the experience of his previous avatar as prime minister. His speeches and interaction with the people demonstrated a maturity and resolve to win the elections. He seemed determined to fulfil all the previous and current promises pledged in the Congress manifesto which had been carefully crafted in consultation with experts.

The singular difference between the earlier Rajiv and the Rajiv of 1991 was a deeper understanding of the diversity of India, the people's aspirations, and the intricacies of politics. Above all, a realization of the negative nexus between the politician, bureaucrat, and industry which was seriously detrimental to the common man. This time around there were no alternative opinions in Delhi's drawing rooms: we were all entirely convinced that Rajiv Gandhi would return with a thumping

majority. Two of my closest friends were often by his side and I was able to grandly announce that I had news straight from the horse's mouth.

The campaign was approaching its last leg and many of the constituencies had already voted by 20 May. Rajiv Gandhi had to return to cast his vote as Delhi was the first to go to the polls that day. The Congress and all Rajiv's

Rajiv Gandhi on the campaign trail (Courtesy: Hindustan Times).

well-wishers, friends, relatives, and especially his family, were relieved that there had been no misadventure because the government had decided, in their collective mean-mindedness, to provide him with minimal security cover. This, even in the face of intelligence reports warning of a threat to his life from vested interests in Punjab, Nagaland, and the Eelam Tigers. The LTTE supremo Velupillai Prabhakaran's hostility to Rajiv was well known in the context of his despatch of an Indian Peace Keeping Force (IPKF) to combat the Tamil Tigers in October 1990. He had indeed called for his head at a meeting held in Jaffna in 1987.

Rajiv's security personnel were devoted and highly motivated but acutely aware of the many loopholes that were impossible to plug given their limited numbers. On 21 May he spent the day campaigning in Orissa, Andhra Pradesh, and Tamil Nadu. The last meeting that night was to be held in a small town on the road between Madras and Kanchipuram. A friend and I were watching the late night news waiting to hear the daily round-up of the elections by a panel of experts. Suddenly a shocked newsreader announced that Rajiv Gandhi had been killed in a bomb explosion at 10.20

p.m. Fourteen others, including a cameraman, had died in that horrifying explosion; among them was Dhanu, a young Tamil woman recruited by the LTTE as a suicide bomber. Utterly shocked and speechless, I sat gazing at the television screen without registering what was being said. I felt that the world around me had suddenly become silent, as every household in India was as stunned as I was.

After a while I suddenly remembered that my friend S was with him. The immediate relief of knowing that he was safe soon turned to guilt as I could not justify my own selfish reaction in the face of such tragedy. Somewhere in that very long 24 hours I heard that the camera of the dead cameraman had been flung some distance but continued to record the events that followed the blast. My mind could only keep replaying this piece of news: a dead man's live camera had remained faithful to its master.

There was collective grief in India, for Rajiv's wife and children and at a personal level. An insurmountable tragedy had struck our nation. For the next 24 hours Delhi was silenced: there were no gatherings of political pundits, no cocktail party chatter. Rajiv was cremated on 24 May at Vir Bhumi, on the banks of the Jamuna beside the memorials of his mother and brother, his young son Rahul performing the last rites.

Death is powerful and final. It resonates fear, sadness, pain, hopelessness, incompleteness. A silent scream rages against what can never return. All that remains of the beloved are memories, which a moment before were invested in a living being. Fifty-two years of independent India had witnessed the death of four members of the Nehru-Gandhi family.

> It takes much more guts and courage to be non-violent than violent.
>
> To my mind the resurgence of communalism is the biggest challenge to national unity.
>
> There are political and religious organizations which continuously ferment fear, insecurity and separatist views — In other words, while the Constitution, the law, the formal political structures point in one direction, elements of social consciousness point in another.
>
> [Rajiv Gandhi]

What if Rajiv Gandhi had not broken journey at Sriperumbudur on 21 May 1991?

- 21 -

The Economic Revolution and Babri Masjid

'Why should the Congress party be hitched to the Nehru-Gandhi family like train compartments to the engine?' inquired Pamulaparti Venkata Narasimha Rao rhetorically.

P.V. Narasimha Rao, as he was popularly called, need not have asked this rhetorical question for two obvious reasons. First, no member of the Congress party would have responded to it; the second, and more important, that Sonia Gandhi, after the tragic death of her husband, wanted to remain completely out of the public eye.

By the mid-1980s, P.V. Narasimha Rao had held no Cabinet position or any Congress party post and had become a postscript in the history of the party. The death of Rajiv Gandhi saw his political fortunes reverse. He was dramatically catapulted centre stage by the Congress party, and anointed as the tenth prime minister of India. He was significantly the first prime minister from south of the Vindhyas and, at the end of his tenure, the first non-Nehru-Gandhi prime minister to complete a full term.

Like many of his predecessors, he inherited a bankrupt exchequer exacerbated by a surge of Hindutva sentiments. The foreign exchange levels had hit rock bottom, particularly after the fall of the Soviet Union. A licence raj, red tape, and large-scale corruption and administrative mismanagement by the previous governments had slowed the GDP to 2-3 per cent. Forty-seven tonnes of India's gold reserves were airlifted overseas as surety for IMF loans.

Narasimha Rao could at this juncture have either maintained the status quo and continued to implement the socialist model instituted by our first prime minister and followed by subsequent governments with minor changes, or he could have introduced radical reforms guaranteeing him unpopularity with his Congress colleagues but essential to save the country from total bankruptcy.

In the face of intense opposition from his party, Narasimha Rao initiated a series of consultations with the IMF. He invited Dr Manmohan Singh to head a committee to formulate economic reforms and embarked on a trajectory of radical changes popularly known as Economic Liberalization led by Manmohan Singh as finance minister. Apart from other significant economic breakthroughs, the reforms led to a phenomenal growth of the IT industry, and India began being referred to as the

Narasimha Rao with Manmohan Singh (Courtesy: Hindustan Times).

information technology hub of the world. A significant number of public sector undertakings were privatized, the licence raj establishment substantially dismantled, state control and red tape significantly reduced, and policies on foreign investment were reworked to attract international investment. The success of all these measures was reflected in a bullish stock market.

The measures adopted to stimulate economic growth brought about a substantial inflow of foreign investment and markedly stemmed the 'brain drain'. By the end of Narasimha Rao's tenure the opening up of the economy saw the return of many prodigal sons who had resigned from well paid jobs and comfortable lifestyles abroad to return home to stake their share in the growing Indian economy. The additional incentives to return to India were domestic help, drivers, and extended families. The markets were flooded with foreign goods, and the wealthy were able to surround themselves with all the trappings of imported luxury which they had hitherto only envied from afar or hesitantly purchased during trips abroad.

There was a sharp rise in the upward mobility of the middle class. Every small town was buzzing with that one or another inspiring success story of a 'local boy' who had made it from rags to riches, a role model to be emulated by those who had yet to experience success. Delhi, in line with other metropolises and smaller cities witnessed the birth of a long chain of people who had become millionaires virtually overnight. Self-employment was the way to go with global markets opening up avenues for small- and mid-sized enterprises. Ancillary or feeder industries were the new buzzwords.

To quote from Jairam Ramesh book *To the Brink and Back* (2015):

> To borrow an analogy from Isaiah Berlin, if Manmohan Singh was the hedgehog who knew only one big thing and that is economic reforms, Rao was the fox who knew many things. It is the fox-hedgehog combine that rescued India in perhaps its darkest moments. India in 1991 could well have mirrored Greece in 2015. That it did not is due to the Narasimha Rao and Manmohan Singh combine.

Then why was the 'fox' not as vigilant on 6 December 1992? On that day, the prime minister of the largest secular democracy in the world slept through the demolition of the secular principles enshrined in the Constitution. His explanation that legally and constitutionally the central government could not at that juncture have imposed President's rule in Uttar Pradesh was unacceptable to most Indians who opposed the demolition of Babri Masjid. Those of us who were not in Ayodhya on 5 and 6 December sat glued to our television sets to witness, horrified, hordes of young, old, and middle-aged Hindus from different professions and varying economic, caste, and class backgrounds, spearheaded by hundreds of sadhus, marching towards the mosque. Down the road from Faizabad they threatened and intimidated Muslims and others along the way who they felt were hostile to them. Their single common goal: teach the Muslims a lesson that they will never forget or erase. It is said that the BJP government of Uttar Pradesh, with Kalyan Singh as its chief minister, was working in cahoots with the RSS and had posted compliant police and administrative officers at Ayodhya and Faizabad to maintain law and order. The *kar sevaks*, spurred by force of numbers, were certainly not confronted by the police or restricted by security arrangements. Rather, they gradually morphing into clones of an unstoppable Frankenstein monster. They had emerged from their camps early on the morning of 6 December and by 6 a.m. had gathered in such vast numbers that all that one could see from a radius of two kilometres was a sea of human heads, many wrapped in saffron turbans or bandanas. They bore aloft saffron flags and, invoking their gods, forming a huge conclave. It was clear that this Frankenstein, the creation of Lal Krishna Advani and company, was in no mood for a mere symbolic act of *kar seva*. Police barricades and cordons were breached and, like the migration of the wildebeest in the Serengeti National Park to the greener pastures of the Maasai Mara National Reserve in Kenya, no force on earth could stop them. They clambered up the three domes like giant carnivorous ants, reducing the age-old mosque to rubble and dust. Muslim houses were burnt, many were brutally assaulted, including the journalists and cameramen who faced the ire of the *kar sevak*s and had their cameras destroyed. All this while the 'supremos' sat comfortably at the site in their viewing chairs gloating and hugging each other at the enactment of a drama they had scripted. Saddened beyond belief, all we could do was gather together at a friend's house that evening and listen to Amir Khusro sung by Nusrat

Hindutva hooligans just prior to the destruction of Babri Masjid, 1992 (Courtesy: The Sahmat Collective).

Fateh Ali with its repetitive 'Ali, Ali, Ali. . .' , the, sonorous breast-beating mourning the death of the Prophet's beloved son-in-law.

The country was divided into 'them' and 'us.' The debate among the pro- and anti-demolition proponents bounced off dhabas, colleges, schools, bus stops, offices, kitty parties, NGOs, human rights advocates, and the drawing rooms of Delhi. Long years of friendship ended, assumptions based on shared ethical values were shattered. I heard many 'liberal' acquaintances exclaim in surprise that they had no Muslim friends, and nostalgically remembered a Muslim girl who had been in school with them, wondering what had become of her.

Riots broke out in many cities of north India. Bombay witnessed the worst communal riots which left 2,000 dead, most of them Muslims, after Bal Thackeray mobilized his Shiva Sena goons to attack their community. The underground Muslim mafia retaliated by engineering a series of bomb blasts. As usual, most of the dead were honest hardworking people with no grudge/enmity towards any community. It led to irreconcilable differences which permitted no closure. The language of politics had turned to hate, destruction, and the vindication of religious identities.

Surely 'personally a good man' Advani, who had witnessed the riots of 1945-47, must have known what the logical conclusion of his *rath yatra* would be? *The Liberhan Commission Report*, ironically commissioned two weeks later by Narasimha Rao, stated that the entire operation had obviously been 'accomplished with phenomenal secrecy, was technically flawless with consistency and assured results ... Leaders know how passions are aroused and how to prevent the same; they

A triumphant Hindutwa mob atop a dome of Babri Masjid,1992 (Courtesy: The Sahmat Collective).

however always see what would be beneficial to them rather than what would be good for the nation. This is what happened in Ayodhya.'

If the BJP believed that this was a sound strategy to win all Hindus of all denominations to its fold post the Mandal agitation, it did not entirely succeed. They did not win sufficient seats in parliament to form a government and had to rely on alliances with other parties in the 1996 parliamentary elections. For that overwhelming victory it had to wait another 18 years when the electorate was won over by tantalizing and illusory promises of development, progress, jobs, and inclusive governance for all its citizens by Narendra Modi. Those promises were alas betrayed by the saffronized India that was heralded by the *rath* yatra, the demolition of Babri Masjid, and the communal poison that is spreading today.

The Congress Party for its part, notwithstanding P.V. Narasimha Rao's resounding success in reforming the Indian economy, suffered its worst electoral defeat to date. Narasimha Rao was the first Indian prime minister, in or out of office, to face a trial on criminal charges and was found guilty in 2000. His conviction was however overturned.

- 22 -

Whither Now

The economic reforms of the early 1990s clearly altered the course of growth and development in India but the seismic event that turbocharged the economy came with a 'geeky' acronym, Y2K, or Year 2000. Technology drove this phenomenon. With the turn of the century, a babel of experts began hyperventilating about the number 2000. After all, dates within computer applications had used the number 1900 since computers were invented. Countless systems were in jeopardy of obsolescence if they failed to convert to 2000 by midnight. Planes would fall out of the sky, power plants grind to a halt, perhaps nuclear missiles would launch of their own volition, banking systems would go bonkers and zero out our accounts, and much else. A veritable doomsday scenario. Every organization employing computer systems set about trying to 'fix' them. Into this scenario rode a group of enterprising Indian 'technogeeks' promising solutions at low prices fuelled by low-cost domestic technology and labour. Companies such as Infosys, Wipro, and Tata Consultancy grew exponentially delivering solutions with competence and quality. Finally, investment in the infrastructure of the vaunted Indian Institutes of Technology was poised to deliver a gigantic return. Thus was born the technology outsourcing industry. From a placid, bucolic military town, Bangalore morphed into our very own Silicon Valley. Manpower was critical in this new paradigm but the key underlying variable was the growth of the Internet, which provided immediate connectivity without the need for physical proximity. The resultant compression of time and space was also a key component of the other tectonic shift, Globalization. The 'Kraken' was unleashed. As the French would proclaim, '*Nous sommes arrive*'.

Incomes accelerated, the middle class expanded, young tech employees travelled globally on assignments, and some settled overseas acquiring experience and expertise that had hitherto been far beyond their reach. Indians were spotted in all the world's great cities, kids in tow, clicking photographs and amassing a host of new memories. Symbols of modern success were furiously acquired: cars, domestic appliances, monstrous TV, sets, and a host of other gizmos. Real estate boomed as we discovered mortgage loans and consumer financing.

What then about our ultra rich? Blatant consumption scaled new heights, quite literally epitomized by the Ambani residence in Mumbai. Twenty-seven floors named Antilia, a mythical island in the Atlantic, overlooking, among other sights, some of the most derelict urban slums in India. Built at a rumoured cost of $2 bn, one can only fantasize about the good that half the construction cost would have yielded had it been devoted to humanitarian causes. Destination weddings, anniversaries, and birthday parties are the norm now for these privileged souls. Bali, Bangkok, Chiang Mai, Singapore and the rest of this glittering earth. 'Want to try something different? How about a Mediterranean cruise for a thousand?' 'Summer in the storied Indian hill stations?' 'Too passé.' 'How about Montreux or Cannes?' London is always an acceptable fallback. Ferraris, Maseratis, and even Lamborghinis prowl the urban streets growling irritably at snail's pace amidst world class traffic jams.

It was not just within our borders that the transformation was occurring. We spread our wings and with globalization driving us into the international arena, we began asserting ourselves in business, leadership, medicine, music, arts, education, and every other conceivable sphere of life. Now when I hear foreign friends casually mentioning that they have just acquired a Jaguar or a Landrover, I remind them they have purchased an 'Indian' car as those two iconic brands are from the Tata Motors stable. The world's largest steel company is Arcelor Mittal, owned and run by an Indian with the humblest of origins. Business leaders from India are proliferating in global companies: Indra Nooyi at Pepsico, Satya Nadela at Microsoft, Sunder Pichai at Google, Ajay Banga at MasterCard, Shantanu Narayan at Adobe Systems, Nikesh Arora at Softbank, Ivan Menezes at Diageo, Ajit Jain at Berkshire Hathaway, to cite a fraction of the list.

We seem to have swamped the market in business education leadership with stalwarts such as Nitin Lohria at Harvard Business School, Sunil Kumar at Chicago Business School, Soumitra Dutta at Cornell, Dipak Jain at

INSEAD where they serve as Deans. There is an emerging domination in the field of medical services. Citizens from developed countries are increasingly flocking to India for treatment and surgeries, motivated by substantially lower costs and excellent outcomes. In the arts, A.R. Rahman won an Oscar for his musical score in *Slum Dog Millionaire*, Reliance Entertainment owns 50 per cent of Dreamworks (Steven Spielberg's 'home' studio), and one of our screen goddesses, Priyanka Chopra, is starring in the hit ABC show *Quantico* on primetime US TV, playing an FBI agent. Let us not forget our most popular export, our cuisine. Gone however are the days of basic currries and naan. There are now a multiplicity of restaurants globally that proudly flaunt the famed Michelin star. The annual San Pellegrino list of the world's 100 best restaurants for 2015 now includes Gaggan in Bangkok at 10, and Indian Accent in my very own hometown, Delhi, at 77.

Amidst all this glitz, glamour, achievement, and high life, the hordes of the needy are still knocking on car windows at traffic intersections, living in hovels, consuming a meal a day, and suffering untold hardship and misery. Infant mortality under the age of five is

5,000 a day, the highest per capita rate in the world. We love those economic statistics mirroring growth-rates, per capita income, foreign direct investment, et al. With China in an economic kerfuffle, we have already proclaimed our place at the high table of the developed nations' club. Really? Once again, a classic case of hubris.

I am not an advocate of choosing one over the other. All I seek is some form of rational equilibrium or are we content to sacrifice a generation of 'have-nots'? When we encourage, support and motivate with the right instruments, we achieve success, and success stories abound. Entrance exam prep schools for the underprivileged that have consistently sent students to élite universities, Indian managers in foreign organizations that outsource and operate in India, IAS and IFS training institutions churning out tomorrow's leaders, graduates of the IIMs climbing the executive ladders in industry. The irony is that most of these prep schools are established by private interests, both domestically and abroad. Just imagine the results were our government to step in and adequately fund a national effort led by an educational technocrat. Add to education, health. We are a nation of 1.3 bn citizens and we harness less than 50 per cent of our human resources. Why is this obvious anomaly not addressed by the Neros that fiddle a tune of secular separatism and majority domination? No easy answers.

No, I am not a pessimist, alarmist, or Chicken Little. I have no prophecy for doom. I just lament the paralytic dysfunctionality that stymies and sucks the life out of dreams. I still have an abiding faith in our spirit and ability to innovate solutions to intractable problems such as water, energy, even global warming. I am less confident about extinguishing the flames of conflict that burn today throughout the world. I am even more despondent about the escalating extremism in our own country. Secularism is firmly embedded in our Constitution but as I have mentioned earlier in this book, the majority's desire to dominate is hard-coded in the societal DNA. Periodically, the spectre of a renewed assault rears up only to be beaten back by a people bound together by common ancestral roots. As the current drumbeat grows louder, so it shall it be, if not silenced, deadened. It is said that Bismarck was among the small minority of leaders who learnt from others' experiences as well as his own. He heeded history's lessons: was aware that we learn from the past, live in the present, for the future. This is somewhat akin to telling your children that your guidance springs from your own life experiences and they are well advised to listen carefully. This sadly is unlikely to occur, bar exceptional cases. Today, it is all about the 'now and here'. What can you say about leaders who have their names stitched all over their suits. My brother called from Seattle, 'Jeez, just saw Modi on TV. Check out his suit closely'. Need I say more.

•

Now, in a more mature and mellow phase of my life, I continue to live in Delhi where I tend to my rooftop garden, enjoy a cup of herb tea every morning while I listen to my favourite arias, followed by a morning constitutional walk. No longer driven by revolutionary, social fervour, I love to cook and travel, and read voraciously. As a professional pursuit, I host dinners for foreign visitors at my home. I thoroughly enjoy introducing them to Indian cuisine and our wayward ways, offering explanations for the apparently incomprehensible sights, sounds, and situations they experience in India. Life is pretty good for the moment. Nikhat and Pratap, my daughter and son-in-law, are settled in London and are nurturing their culinary business, hosting a well-received gourmet supper club, and producing gourmet food products. My elder brother and Nancy are retired in Seattle and making preparations to welcome their first grandchild. My aunt in London still sees patients at age 86 and mentors students, and a cousin in Zurich tends to his wonderful family. Last but not least, my *khandan* of friends continue to fill my daily life with laughter and love.

Growing up, my father once asked us, 'If you had a choice, would you go back to the past for one day or forward to the future?" My brothers chose the future but I chose the past. Yes, I would like to return to a Delhi when civility and kindness were the norm. A time when we actually admired our political leaders, when materialism and malls were not the centre of lives, and secularism was in large part the governing political philosophy. A time when religious fundamentalism was not fanning an ill wind across our land. Was it not Lord Alfred Tennyson who wrote in *Ulysses*, 'The old order changeth, yielding place to the new, lest one good

custom corrupt the world'? Perhaps the Lord (Tennyson) assumed the new order too would be for the good. I fervently hope that will be the case.

Nikhat and Pratap's wedding celebration in London, 2013 (Courtesy: Jonathan Page).

Copyright Declaration

I have endeavoured to recreate events, locales, and conversations from my memories of them. In order to maintain their anonymity, in some instances I have changed the names of individuals and places, and some identifying characteristics and details such as physical appearance, occupation, and place of residence.

Although the author and publisher have made every effort to ensure that the information in this book was correct when it went to press, they do not assume and hereby disclaim any liability to any party for any loss, damage, or disruption caused by errors or omissions, whether such errors or omissions result from negligence, accident, or any other cause.

In particular, I would like to acknowledge, with thanks, the following authors from whom I have borrowed ideas, quotations, and photographs: Sheba Chhachhi, Ram Rahman, The Sahmat Collective, Raj and Helen Rewal, Gujral Foundation, Jairam Ramesh, Masseh Rahman, Tejbir Singh, Master Tara Singh, Omar Khayyam.